YAZOO

Integration in a Deep-Southern Town

WILLIE MORRIS

NEW EDITION

The University of Arkansas Press
Fayetteville

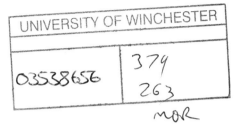
Copyright © 1971, 2012 by The University of Arkansas Press
First edition 1971. Second edition 2012.

ISBN-10: 1-55728-983-2
ISBN-13: 978-1-55728-983-4

16   15   14   13   12   5   4   3   2   1

LIBRARY OF CONGRESS CATALOGING-IN-PUBLICATION DATA

Morris, Willie.
    Integration in a deep-southern town / Willie Morris.
— New ed.
        p.   cm.
    Includes bibliographical references.
    ISBN 978-1-55728-983-4 (pbk. : alk. paper)
    1. Segregation in education—Mississippi—Yazoo City.
    2. Yazoo City (Miss.)—Race relations. I. Title.
LC212.522.M57.M67   2012
379.2'630976249—dc23
                                2012005190

To David

CONTENTS

INTRODUCTION

Willie Morris's *Yazoo: Integration in a Deep-Southern Town*, which appeared in book form in 1971, originated as a long article published in *Harper's Magazine* in 1970 under the intriguing title "Yazoo . . . notes on survival." Morris was guaranteed wide readership for both versions of this personalized account of how his hometown of Yazoo City, Mississippi, dealt with the social crisis brought about by court-ordered school integration. By the time they appeared in print he had already made a name for himself as the youngest ever editor-in-chief of the prestigious *Harper's Magazine*. However, despite the significance of the topic, Morris was reluctant to make what promised to be an emotionally difficult journey back home to report on the event. He tells his readers, using italics for emphasis, simply, *"I did not want to go."*[1] Readers of *Yazoo* may be initially surprised by the rawness of Morris's emotions, by the intensity of his desire to escape what he regarded as his fate to be a cultural interpreter and a witness of how Mississippi responded to the social changes brought about by the African American civil rights movement.

While grappling with the decision of whether or

not to write *Yazoo,* his reluctance stemmed in part from the fact that he had already written a book set in his hometown and had lived with the fallout from trying to tell the imperfect truth about people and a place that he loved. In 1967, his compelling memoir of southern boyhood, *North Toward Home,* had been published to much interest and acclaim among the nation's intelligentsia. *Publisher's Weekly* noted the book's "fine quality, humor, perception," and in the pages of the *Wall Street Journal,* John O'Connor deemed it a "sensitive and affecting portrait."[2] Despite the national praise it garnered, the book had been received with ambivalence if not hostility by many in Morris's hometown.

He had written about life in small-town Mississippi during the 1940s and 1950s with nostalgia and tenderness, proclaiming, "I knew Mississippi and I loved what I saw . . . Each street and hill was like a map of my consciousness; I loved the contours of its land, and the slow changing of its seasons."[3] But like any good memoirist, he also gave insights into many darker aspects of his place of origin and of his own character. Many of these revelations centered on the region's notoriously poor race relations and pervasive socioeconomic inequalities. Showing a remarkable willingness to lay himself bare, he early on accepted as a truism a belief that would influence his later writing; namely, that "an autobiography that does not tell something bad about the author cannot be any good."[4] He confessed, for example, to having succumbed to the tendency toward violence he considered endemic to the region. Brutality was, after all, a necessary component of maintaining the racial caste system.

One day when he was twelve years old, acting out of blind instinct and without deliberation, Morris hid in some shrubs, pounced on an African American toddler who was walking by with this older sister, and kicked and shoved the little boy. Although he later was ashamed of his actions, they sprang from what he regarded as a collective sense that "the Negroes in the town were *there:* they were ours to do with as we wished."[5] Many white residents of Yazoo City were understandably sensitive about having these kinds of regional sins analyzed and exposed to a national audience by one of their own. *North Toward Home* left some segments of the white population feeling exposed and betrayed.

Morris wrote about the local response to his memoir in *Yazoo*, which some readers regarded as a sequel of sorts to the earlier book. Lew Powell of the *Delta Democrat Times*, in fact, speculated that a "more accurate subtitle might have been Afterthoughts on North Toward Home."[6] Critical letters were published in the local newspaper; Morris's mother received threatening phone calls; and the young author was warned never to return home.[7] Although others were proud of his accomplishments or flattered to be memorialized as characters in a book destined to become a literary classic, Morris still recalled feeling "trepidation over what I had done." He agonized, wondering if he had hurt Yazoo City, repeatedly asking himself, "Had I dealt with it honestly? Had I been true to it, and to myself?"[8]

Because of these complicated emotions and his ambivalent attitude toward home, which was unambiguously captured in the title of his "autobiography in mid-passage," he was understandably reluctant to once again write about Yazoo City.[9] He was propelled southward again in the wake of the 1969 Supreme Court ruling in *Alexander v. Holmes*, which added concrete urgency to the court's notoriously vague 1955 mandate that desegregation of public schools should take place with "all deliberate speed." At long last, fifteen years after school desegregation had technically become the law of the land with the landmark *Brown* decision, the October 1969 *Alexander* ruling forbade any further delays. Thirty-three Mississippi school districts, including Yazoo City, were ordered to "terminate dual school systems at once." They were to reopen on an integrated basis after the winter recess that very year.

The changes brought by the court's decision were dramatic. In Mississippi, 67,000 black students and 56,000 white students would shift schools at midyear. The rest of the state's schools were required to comply by the fall 1970 semester.[10] For Morris, a longtime critic of the southern racial order who was perpetually torn between feeling happily displaced and homesick while he lived in New York, the lure of the human drama about to unfold in Yazoo City proved to be both irresistible and terrifying. He ultimately decided to go and bear witness "because the urge to be there during Yazoo's most critical moment was too elemental to resist, and because I would have been ashamed of myself if I had not."[11]

Yazoo City had been notoriously intransigent on the issue of school integration in the past, a history that Morris knew well and felt deeply. As a college student visiting home for spring break, he had attended an early meeting of the Yazoo City Citizens' Council in 1955. The organization had been founded in Indianola, Mississippi, the previous year for the primary purpose of providing organized resistance to the Supreme Court's *Brown* decision. Although the Citizens' Council organization spread to other regions of the South, Mississippi was and remained, in the words of the historian Neil McMillen, the "mother of the movement."[12]

Yazoo City formed an early and especially enthusiastic chapter of the organization. The meeting that Morris attended had been called to develop a strategy to deal with the fact that fifty-three local African Americans had signed a petition asking for the desegregation of the public school system. His community's response to their black neighbors' request for equal access to educational resources was shocking to Morris, so much so that he wrote about the event in *North Toward Home*, *Yazoo*, and in *The Ghosts of Medgar Evers*, a book that was published more than three decades after the first installment of his autobiography and twenty-seven years after the publication of *Yazoo*. That traumatic experience was one that would not easily fade from his memories.

Morris was stunned to see community leaders and other adults he had known and respected since his childhood leading the charge against not only the idea of school integration but also against the specific individuals who had signed the petition. Collectively they determined that the white community would band together to fire from their jobs those who signed the document and evict them from their rental properties.[13] Banks refused to let the protestors deposit their money. Grocers and other merchants vowed not to sell them supplies.[14] Morris was particularly shaken when one local citizen who dared question the constitutionality of such measures was booed and hissed at by the hysterical crowd. He wondered, *"Who are these people?"* and "What was I doing there?"[15]

The tactics of his neighbors, which horrified Morris, were incredibly effective. The Citizens' Council put an advertisement in the *Yazoo City Herald* listing the names of those who had signed the petition to be sure that local whites would have no doubt as to whom they should penalize. In the aftermath, fifty petitioners asked to have their names removed from the document. Of the three remaining signers, two left town permanently as did even some of those who asked that their names be stricken from the list.[16]

Bolstered by their success, the Citizens' Council continued to grow and had 1,500 local members by September 1955. This figure was particularly impressive given the fact that the town had a population of only 11,000 people at the time.[17] The white resistance to the encroachments of the civil rights movement appeared to many to be nearly universal. Morris was hardly surprised when he later heard that state NAACP field secretary Medgar Evers once told the national office "for Yazoo City there doesn't seem to be much hope."[18]

Instead, Yazoo City took a tactic favored by many southern communities who were determined to resist desegregation, and they began to concentrate on equalizing the educational opportunities that they provided for the town's black and white citizens. They hoped that raising the pay of black teachers and building better facilities for black pupils would soften African American agitation for integration. The attempt to equalize the school systems was greeted with ambivalence by white Mississippians who never fully funded these programs. As the historian Charles C. Bolton notes, the plan was fundamentally flawed in large part because "the equalization of two separate school systems would never succeed in a state that did not even have the resources to adequately fund one group of schools."[19]

Although the Yazoo City school system was willing to make meaningful strides toward greater equality between the separate school systems, in 1955 the idea of school desegregation remained out of the question. A survey of the city's school system prepared in 1955 by H. M. Ivy, founder of Associated Consultants in Education and former Yazoo City public teacher, unabashedly declared:

> We believe that a continuation of segregation in Mississippi irrespective of whether it is maintained by law is not only possible but necessary for the best development of each group . . . The development of the Negro has been remarkable but taken as a whole the Negro as found in Mississippi . . . has not reached the development in transition that causes him to be willing to undergo the self-discipline, application and trust in the future benefits that is incumbent upon many of the white man's ways, particularly his education.[20]

The local rationale for and commitment to separate schools could hardly have been made clearer than in Ivy's report. The city successfully staved off desegregation until 1967. The previous year, the Department of Health, Education, and Welfare had utilized the power given to it under the Civil Rights Act of 1964 to cut off federal funding to school systems that had failed to develop a school integration program and had withheld federal monies from the school system. Yazoo City responded by reluctantly allowing school desegregation by the "freedom-of-choice" plan that was adopted by many school systems throughout the South.[21] Theoretically, these programs gave children the choice of whether or not they wanted to attend their color-segregated neighborhood schools or to participate in a limited integration effort. However, cumbersome bureaucratic procedures, discouragement on the part of local officials, and pressure from the white power establishment discouraged most black children from opting to participate.

In *Yazoo* Morris reported that as late as 1969, fewer than one hundred black children were attending white majority schools in the town. Gloria Owens, one of the black students who elected to participate in this program, later recalled being humiliated and terrorized while attending the white junior high school beginning in 1968. Among other abusive actions, her white classmates allowed a German shepherd to attack her. Both her fellow students and her teachers conspired together to make her feel so uncomfortable and so unwelcome that she recalled that going to school "was like torture, it was like being in prison."[22]

Well aware of this history, Morris responded with interest and anxiety to the news that his hometown was about to come to terms with the kind of meaningful school integration it had fought so desperately to avoid. In an early draft of the *Harper's Magazine* article he confessed that it was not the "overwhelming psychic urges of the writer" that led him there.[23] As the novelist and journalist Dan Wakefield noted in his *New York Times* review of *Yazoo*, Morris had to contend with the fact that to the reading public, "Social problems are essentially boring." The right-leaning electorate that had ushered Richard Nixon into office with their search for law and order along with many white nominal defenders of the civil rights movement were, Wakefield suggests, "tired of Mississippi."[24] In the aftermath of significant legislative victories in the form of the Civil Rights Act of 1964 and the Voting Rights Act of 1965, many considered the civil rights movement to be over. The new political landscape brought about by the emergence of Black Power and black urban rebellions in the mid-1960s was unsettling to many white Americans who in bewilderment abandoned even a tepid commitment to the continued struggle for racial equality. Morris had no reason to assume that the social transformation that was shaking Yazoo City would interest the rest of the country as deeply as it moved him, a truth that made it even more incumbent upon him to utilize the platform his position at *Harper's Magazine* gave him, to make people care, and once again to serve as a cultural ambassador between the flawed Mississippi that he loved and a wider world.

Propelled in part by what Fred Hobson has labeled

the "southern rage to explain," he went to bear witness and to chronicle this moment in his town's history even though he did so carrying the burden of the premonition that *Some bastard is going to kill me in Yazoo.*"[25] Although his fear was fueled by memories of the "unthinking sadism" of he and his childhood friends and the uncomfortable local reception of *North Toward Home*, it was also, he later realized, the outgrowth of an even deeper psychological worry, that of having "too deep an involvement in this place."[26]

As a young man Morris left his native state to attend college at the University of Texas and then to study at Oxford University as a Rhodes Scholar. After completing his education, he briefly worked as editor of the progressive *Texas Observer* before he was lured northward to New York City to become what J. Speed Carroll flippantly but accurately described as "a practicing member of the intelligentsia."[27] It had been a mind-bogglingly rapid transformation, and the early years he spent in New York were heady. In *New York Days*, the 1993 sequel to *North Toward Home*, Morris captured with undiminished surprise and glee what that experience was like remembering, "There were eight million telephone numbers in the Manhattan directory, and every one of them would have returned my calls."[28] He tried desperately to actualize the title of the first volume of his autobiography, to transform New York into home. He developed strong friendships with other writers, many of them southern transplants like himself, and thrived on the exhilaration of living in such a densely and diversely populated place. He thrilled at expanding his horizons, relishing each new sensation: "The provincial once inured to catfish, fried squirrel, and cornbread soaked in buttermilk took to the enlivening Jewish delis . . . the bagels and lox and gefilte fish, the prolific fragrances of them."[29]

New York was, however, also the site of a great deal of pain for Morris, who saw his first marriage dissolve in 1969. His growing sense of rootlessness increased in 1971 when, after a dispute with the owners of *Harper's Magazine* over finances, editorial content, and the future direction of the magazine, Morris resigned his position in disgust. As the title of the final chapter of *New York Days* reveals, despite the charms of the city, Morris never truly felt he belonged there. Ultimately he recognized the inevitable and headed "South Toward Home" to become an instructor and visiting writer at the University of Mississippi in 1980.

When Willie Morris traveled to Yazoo City in 1970 to watch the saga of school integration unfold, he had not yet made this geographical reversal, and he was more intensely engaged than ever with this lifelong struggle to define his relationship to the South. In 1964, Morris had an epiphany, which permanently shaped the way he thought about his native state. He was at dinner with a group of civil rights activists who told him news about their struggles to change the racial climate in Mississippi. During the course of the meal, one of the women he was dining with began sobbing and left the table without explanation. One of his companions explained that she had never before socialized with a white person from Mississippi. Given the brutal associations she had about white Mississippians, this interaction had made her "nervous as hell." Then and there Morris had a realization that in retrospect must have seemed obvious to him. Suddenly he understood:

> The Mississippi these young people talked of was a different place from the one I had known, the things they said were not in context with mine; it was as if we were talking of another world—one that *looked* the same, that had the same place names, the same roads and rivers and landmarks, but beyond that the reality was awry, removed from my private reality of it.[30]

For Morris, thoughts of Mississippi would hereafter always be accompanied by a tortured set of the painful dualities. His subjective experiences of a relatively carefree, joyful childhood where he was blissfully "pleasant, enthusiastic, and happy" contrasted starkly with the realities faced by African American children of his same age bracket.[31] The color line was so rigid and the differing sets of expectations and opportunities so fixed, that indeed they were talking about different places.[32]

He later reflected that his Mississippi was full of "paradoxes," which were perhaps most aptly expressed in Yazoo City, "sitting there on the precipice of the great Delta flatland." He mused:

> Its rough-hewn democracy, complicated by all the visible textures of caste and class, encompassed harmless boyhood fun right along with all sorts of treacheries and tensions and deceits: murders and other lesser transgressions, rank hypocrisies, church-going sanctimonies, unrepentant avarice, and above all, I would someday grow to see, racial hatred and calculated repression.[33]

To a great extent Willie Morris's life and his work —both his nonfiction writing and his later novels— were devoted to untangling the complexities of these two different Mississippis, of explaining their uneasy coexistence both to himself and to his readers. Ultimately, he hoped to help dissolve the distance between them, longing for the advent of a new Mississippi, one recognizable to and inhabited by both white and black people. This dream is why he greeted the integration of the Yazoo City schools with such hopeful enthusiasm.

The dualities that Morris saw in Mississippi, which

painfully informed his memories of the place, were also manifested in his own psyche. One of the phrases in *Yazoo* quoted most frequently by reviewers of the book was Morris's tortured confession, "One of the more perplexing ironies of my life is that the longer I live in Manhattan, the more Southern I seem to become, the more obsessed with the old warring impulses of one's sensibility to be both Southern and American."[34] This carefully chosen description of the rift he felt in his own identity did not appear in the first drafts of the piece for *Harper's Magazine* but was penciled onto the margins of one of his heavily edited versions of the manuscript.[35] The phrase appeared in the *Harper's Magazine* article fairly early on in the essay, in section 4, which begins with the observation that upon seeing Yazoo City again after his northern exile he realized:

> The town has changed remarkably little in twenty years, and as I drive these streets which are a map on my consciousness, I see the familiar places—the hills and trees and houses—in a strange, dreamlike quality, as if what I am seeing here is not truly real, but faintly blurred images caught in my imagination from a more pristine time.[36]

This passage again captures Morris's growing awareness of the existence of competing versions of Mississippi, the nostalgic one from his childhood memories and the darker one that he had been able to see more clearly from the distance of New York and through the perceptions of the young civil rights workers. The town had a surreal quality to Morris because he realized that his memories were partial, incomplete, distorted. As deeply ingrained as Yazoo City was in his sense of identity, he realized he would never have complete knowledge of the place, that the Yazoo City of his imagination was inhabited only by him.

In the book *Yazoo*, Morris moved the carefully wrought phrase "to be both Southern and American" from the beginning of the piece nearer to the end, as a more final assessment of what his return to Yazoo had taught him about himself. The relocation of the phrase demonstrates the workings of a careful, deliberative writer mindful about how he portrayed both the historical events he had observed and the impact those events had on him.

Throughout his work, Morris was unusually candid about his relationship to the text. Although he strove to be fair to his subject, he made no pretense toward some kind of absolute objectivity, knowing that the writer's thoughts and emotions—even those of a skilled, well-trained journalist like himself—could never be separated from his work. After all, social realities, while established collectively, are ultimately experienced as individuals.[37] His Mississippi was colored by his growing awareness of its dualities and by his increasing understanding of his own divided sensibilities and allegiances. In the acknowledgments to *Yazoo*, he clarified his point of view, proclaiming, "This volume by no means pretends to be a 'definitive' study of my native state during the year following massive racial integration . . . Rather it is one writer's very personal view."[38]

The book version of *Yazoo* contained an extended meditation on what it meant to Morris to be a southerner and a resident New Yorker, which was not included in the *Harper's* article. Much of his rumination was centered on how much he admired the magazine, which had become a symbol to him of things "American" as opposed to "Southern." He gloried in the fact that each issue contained items that "would be read a hundred years hence."[39] In contrast, in *North Toward Home* he had bemoaned the fact that while his southern boyhood encouraged him to cultivate an active imagination, he had grown up in a place "where more specific exercises in intellection— like reading books—were not accepted."[40] Thus his American and southern dichotomy was in part a divide between head and heart. The people in New York, he proclaimed, "would not allow you to go stale," but the South was an unshakable "feeling in the blood."[41] He had chosen New York and all that it represented, but the South had chosen him and would not let him go.

Morris's formulation of being "both Southern and American" contains echoes—perhaps even deliberate ones—of the venerable African American intellectual W. E. B. Du Bois's penetrating description of his own "two-ness," of being both "an American, a Negro; two souls, two thoughts, two unreconciled strivings."[42] Morris would have been appropriately cautious about conflating his own experiences with those of an African American who did not have his same racial privileges, but the Du Boisian idea of "double consciousness," a concept that has a long line of intellectual antecedents ranging from Ralph Waldo Emerson to William James, may have partially resonated with him.[43] Although he would never know the sting of racism, he did know the lesser sensation of feeling perpetually displaced. As a native son of a much-maligned region, he too may have become accustomed to "measuring one's soul by the tape of a world that looks on in amused contempt and pity."[44] Indeed sometimes Morris himself, the sophisticated New Yorker, surveyed his younger self, his other self through that gaze. But just as Du Bois felt that a split identity, a feeling of being marginalized and partially outside both worlds, gave African Americans "a second-sight in this American world," Morris, too, relished the perspectival blessing of his divided identity.[45] The view was clearer from the margins.

Later in his life after he left New York to return to Mississippi, he articulated what it meant to interpret his home state from a divided viewpoint:

> [W]hen a writer knows home in his heart, his
> heart must remain subtly apart from it. He
> must always be a stranger to the place he
> loves, and its people. His claim to home is
> deep, but there are too many ghosts. He must
> absorb without being absorbed. When he
> understands, as few others do, something of
> his home in America—Mississippi—that is
> funny, or sad, or cruel or beautiful, or true, he
> knows he must do so as a stranger.[46]

It is this simultaneous closeness and writerly distance that makes Morris's *Yazoo* so compelling and so unique in the vast literature surrounding school integration. The desegregation of the public schools in the South captured the national imagination in a way that few other aspects of the civil rights struggle could. For as the historian Rebecca de Schweinitz argues, "While the nation was willing to sit by and watch black men and women suffer under Jim Crow, it was less willing to accept children encountering the same discrimination and hostility."[47] Black and white photographs of perfectly attired, somber African American students courageously facing jeering, spitting white mobs are seared into our national memory. That same national memory, however, is too frequently inhabited by stock characters. Those children are remembered as long-suffering saints, and rightfully so, but they are also flash-frozen in time with little thought to what impact their heroism had on their lives and their communities or how they managed to process the disconnect brought about by another kind of two-ness, American ideals about equality and American hate-ridden actualities. They are juxtaposed on the other side with Governor George Wallace physically barring entrance to the University of Alabama; Governor Ross Barnett allowing Oxford, Mississippi, to dissolve into chaos; and Governor Orval Faubus ordering the National Guard to aid him in defying the Supreme Court's desegregation mandate.

These memories compromise a large part of what Brian Ward has labeled the "master narrative" of the civil rights movement.[48] One of the elements missing from this tale of larger-than-life monsters and saints is the vast realm in between. These kinds of oversimplifications are not found in *Yazoo*. As Jonathan Yardley aptly observed, "Morris offers no heroes or villains, no easy answer—only people struggling with more good will and hope than might be expected, to meet a social crisis."[49]

Morris excelled in capturing the humanity of his subjects. In what many critics labeled the most stirring section of the book, Morris profiled a number of individuals involved in the saga of school integration, both supporters and opponents of the court order, both white and black. Given Morris's strong desire to see the integration of Yazoo City's schools happen peacefully and successfully, the seeming detachment

with which he described the different local viewpoints on the issue is remarkable. His restraint ele-
vates the book from becoming a polemic on the
virtues of integration, making it instead a compelling
historical document and one of the richest and most
multi-perspectival accounts we have of a community's attempt to come to terms with the realities of
seismic social change. Morris—who straightfor-
wardly and continuously reminded his readers of his
presence in the text and his relationship to the subject matter—strove to make observations about
rather than to pass judgments on the people he inter-
views. He endeavored to allow individual observers
to speak for themselves, capturing their thoughts
with what the editor of the *Yazoo City Herald*
Norman Mott called "a tape recorder ear." Morris,
Mott claimed, should be thought of as a "literary historian" who used his skills as a keen observer and a
master of the English language to capture nuanced
aspects of a now-vanished historical moment.[50]

Yazoo brings together the journalistic rigor and literary style of the New Journalism to create a generic
hybrid. It is part reportage, part memoir, part ethnog-
raphy, part social critique. Morris captured a cacoph-
onous array of responses to the moment, ranging from
Mayor Jeppie Barbour's lament that the town's African
American citizens were "goin' through a state of being
rebellious and hard-nosed not listenin' to white people
like they used to" to pro-integrationist grocery store

owner and rare white NAACP member David "Deacon" Pattenote's hope that the town's black young people both literally and metaphorically would not "allow that big ole bus to pass 'em by any more."[51] One of the most fascinating voices that he recorded was that of Rudy Shields, a local civil rights leader and staunch advocate for school desegregation.

Morris described Shields as "very black, self-assured, well-built, and outwardly mean-tempered (but not as mean as he may think he is)." He allowed space in the text for Shields to describe his strategies of black activism and his assessment of the situation in Yazoo City in his own voice. Morris introduced Shields by acknowledging that he is "anathema," a "devil" to the white community but then surprised his readers by allowing his subject to speak for himself. His voice as captured by Morris exudes far more faith in the community than the reader expects.[52] "Yazoo," Shields said in agreement with his interlocutor, "has great potential."[53]

When Shields arrived in Yazoo City, he was already a seasoned civil right activist who had, by his own count, been involved in thirty other boycott campaigns.[54] He had gained a reputation for fearlessness. Stories abounded about him returning fire when a group of whites shot at him, casually entering spaces that had been long segregated by local customs, and generally comporting himself without manifesting subservience or fear even in the presence of the most outspoken racists.

Shields, who came to Mississippi from Chicago to participate in civil rights work there, collaborated closely with Charles Evers, the older brother of the Mississippi civil rights martyr Medgar Evers, and the two developed a model of protest that they implemented in a number of Mississippi towns in the late 1960s in an attempt to wrest concessions from communities that had remained largely intransigent to black pleas for greater equality even after the passage of landmark federal civil rights legislation in 1964 and 1965.[55] Local activists would draft a list of demands that would be delivered to the white power structure and would commence a boycott of white-owned businesses until their requests were met. Although specific concerns might vary from community to community, they generally involved issues such as school integration, black employment opportunities, and living conditions in black neighborhoods.

These boycotts were bolstered by the efforts of paramilitary groups who were pledged to protect black protesters and who, according to the historian Emilye Crosby, "wanted to heighten white fears by making the existing self-defense efforts more visible and explicitly threatening."[56] Their efforts would be further supported by a corollary group of black activists pledged to enforcing the boycott in their own community. In Yazoo City, these enforcers became known as "the spirit."[57] Black Mississippian Ed Cole described how groups like "the spirit" functioned: "Folks go shop, break the boycott, they didn't get home with the damn groceries . . . cause somebody was waiting for them when they got there."[58]

Shields successfully employed these tactics in Yazoo City as he built upon a tradition of black activism in the community. They issued a list of twenty-five demands and began a rigidly enforced boycott of white businesses.[59] Shields began establishing a reputation as someone who was not afraid of the local power establishment. He openly armed himself and wrote a strident letter to the editor in the *Yazoo City Herald*, in which he declared, "Our philosophy, I am not speaking for the NAACP, but for the Black people in general, is 'if you kill our cat, we'll get your dog,' this is no threat but a promise."[60] These tactics had the desired effect of scaring and agitating the white community. A letter writer to the *Yazoo City Herald* angrily described nameless boycott leaders, in what was likely a thinly disguised dig at Shields, as "pussyfooting, goateed Yahoos, unshaven and their hippie attire from Chicago, New York, Detroit, Etc." and begged local African Americans to not allow this "bunch of punks" to weaken "your relations with your friends and neighbors."[61] Marion Morris, Willie Morris's mother, wrote a letter to her son articulating her disdain for Rudy Shields and begging him to "*weigh* very carefully what you *quote* and write about Rudy Shields in your piece . . . I simply cannot take any more criticisms as in the past in the papers." She reported that Viola, the African American maid whom the family had employed for many years, was terrified to violate the boycott so Marion Morris had bought chicken feed for her and brought home shoes for her to try on.[62] Tellingly, none of the white community's vitriol against Shields found its way into Morris's evenhanded account of his activities.

Although Morris endeavored to record a number of voices of black members of the community, including those of black students who were part of the integration experiment, he faced criticism for allegedly caring too much about the white perspective of the event. The historian William F. Holmes claimed that one of the weaknesses of *Yazoo* was that it was "written almost totally from the point of view of the whites, focusing upon their fears, hopes, adjustments . . . Morris is not sufficiently sensitive to the problems of blacks."[63] This criticism was repeated by Mel Leventhal, a lawyer for the NAACP Legal Defense Fund, who worked for the cause of school desegregation in Mississippi and whom Morris wrote warmly about in *Yazoo*. When asked about this criticism in an interview in 1980, Morris matter of factly responded, "Well, I am white. I suppose the bias is inevitable."[64] One could also argue that the "bias" Morris described is also perhaps *desirable*. In addition to memorably recording the reactions of a wide variety of other Yazoo City residents to the issue, he provided his readers with extended insights into his own emotional responses, his own perceptions about the significance of the moment. His point of view as someone who was both in favor of integration and who also understood the fears and anxieties of those who oppose it is one that is frequently missing from the historical record, which often overlooks layered emotions. Morris's skill as a writer gives his readers the opportunity to experience different points of view and to visit temporarily and imaginatively different Mississippis just as he did.

For all of his concern about the state of race relations in his native state and his desire to use his writing in part to ameliorate some of these tensions, Morris was not guilty of a condescending sense of *noblesse oblige* toward the black community. Throughout his life he felt compelled to use his skills as a writer in the cause of social justice. He once remarked, "I never marched in demonstrations. I was not, for instance, at Selma, where some of my friends marched, but I felt that my writing was my main responsibility in that regard."[65] He wrote not to advise black people on how they should go about fighting for civil rights, but instead much of his work was aimed at explaining to the white community why this was necessary and how corrosive racism was to everyone.

Morris wrote *Yazoo* not long after conversations

about the role of whites in the civil rights movement had begun to dominate many conversations among activists working in the South, most notably among members of the Student Nonviolent Coordinating Committee (SNCC), some of whom were acquaintances of Morris. Ultimately, in December 1966 members narrowly voted to expel white activists from the organization.[66] One of the driving factors behind the expulsion vote was a growing resentment toward whites who were too quick to assume leadership positions at the expense of African Americans who were, by the nature of their identity, more closely tied to the struggle. Furthermore, many black members of the civil rights movement observed that even the most sympathetic white ally was sometimes not aware enough of his or her own white privilege.[67]

Mindful of these tensions and potential pitfalls as a white southerner writing about race, Morris claimed ultimately to speak only for himself, a position that by no means indicated a lack of empathy or curiosity about the black experience. In an article published in *Dissent* in 1963 Morris reflected on the violence that erupted in 1962 in a failed attempt to prevent African American James Meredith from enrolling at the University of Mississippi. Morris confessed to his readers, "I write about Mississippi with an almost total despair." In solving the crisis of racism that embroiled his state, Morris did not, however, look to white liberals to solve the problem on behalf of a grateful black population. Instead he articulated a vision of black empowerment:

> The hope for racial justice in the Southern states most assuredly does not lie in some imaginary curing of the Southern split personality . . . Nor does it lie, as other white Southern liberals vaguely suggest, in the forging in fire, with each passing crisis, of the white man's psyche. I am more concerned with what happens to Meredith's psyche, and others like him. It lies primarily, as a first step, in the Negro vote. Without the vote, all those goals which the Negro, with his white ally, has set for himself remain politically inaccessible; with it the Negro can become less and less a ward of the white man.[68]

Although he may not have thought of it that way, Morris was agreeing with certain aspects of the Black Power philosophy that had not yet been fully articulated when his article appeared. Black Power argued for the prime importance of black electoral power and also of the dire necessity of realizing that the racial divide though regrettable was real. White allies of the black struggle had to understand that although each bore the psychic wounds of racism, their scars were not identical or of equal severity.

Morris felt a deep affinity for southern African Americans with whom he shared many cultural traits. However, he was careful not to let these feelings of similarity and closeness grow into presumption, and he kept a respectful distance when it mattered most. In *Yazoo* he mentions feeling a strong kinship with African American writer Alice Walker, who was then married to Mel Leventhal. He remarked, "She is a Southerner—and in fact reminds me a little of myself."[69] His feeling of cultural similarity and belonging with black writers Ralph Ellison and Albert Murray was even stronger. In *North Toward Home* Morris recalls feeling the most at home he had ever felt in New York at a New Year's Eve meal of "bourbon, collard greens, black-eyed peas, ham-hocks, and cornbread" that he shared with them. He credits both men with helping him learn not to "betray [his] own unique consciousness as a white Southern intellectual from Yazoo City."[70] However, despite these intense connections, he was also realistically aware of moments of inevitable distance. Reflecting on the "merging . . . of the great European and African sources" in Mississippi while he was growing up, he also noted somewhat sadly that "we belonged together and yet did not, the barrier between us acute and invisible. It was very strange and hard."[71] Although he empathized and considered himself an ally with the black freedom struggle, he did not have the temerity to speak from any subject position other than his own.

For Morris and for others of his ilk, the terrain of the late civil rights movement was tricky to navigate.

Stokely Carmichael, who was elected SNCC chairman in 1966, declared integration "irrelevant" that same year, a stance that proved to be somewhat bewildering for many who had, like Morris, been committed to the goal of desegregation for many years. As a child, Morris accepted the racial realities of his region and in fact as a fourteen-year-old wrote an editorial for the *Flashlight*, his school newspaper, defending Strom Thurmond, the Dixiecrats, and the "Mississippi Way of Life."[72] He began to challenge the unthinking conservativism and racism of his youth while at college at the University of Texas. While he was there, the landmark *Brown* decision caused him to begin to rethink his basic assumptions. In December 1954, he wrote an article for the student newspaper, the *Daily Texan*, entitled "Best Solution Must Be Slow," where he advocated a "patient and comradely approach to the problem."[73] By the time he ran for the editorship of the paper in 1955, he was on record as being in favor of desegregation of the university, saying, "I don't think Ole Miss is ready for integration. I think the University of Texas is."[74] By December 1955, Morris's column was optimistically predicting, "It is in the colleges and universities of the South that the 'second class citizenship' of the Negro will initially be eradicated."[75] He later continued to cover the issue as editor of the *Texas Observer*, where he sarcastically reported on the decision of Boerne, Texas, not to integrate their schools, noting wryly that the "good old keep 'em in their place philosophy was upheld by that touchstone of all else, the democratic process."[76]

In 1967, Morris traveled to Yazoo City for National Library Week, giving speeches at both the white and the black high schools. In what was likely one of the most unusual assemblages of personalities the town had ever seen, he brought William Styron, Larry L. King, and Norman Podhoretz with him. At the black high school he gave what must have been one of the most frank speeches the black majority audience had ever heard a white Mississippian make. In passages drawn directly from the manuscript of *North Toward Home*, he unflinchingly admitted to his childhood racism, confessing, for example, to the incident when he kicked and injured the African American toddler. His friend Harriet DeCell thought she noticed some discomfort on Morris's part and wondered why he was telling those painful stories in that setting. However, she later speculated that he was "exorcising a deep, complex, soul-searing guilt sense." She wondered, "Can a speech at a Negro high school really atone for anything?"[77]

Although atonement may have been part of his purpose, he was also likely attempting once again to bridge the racial divide, to bring the competing Mississippis together by giving the African American students gathered there a glimpse inside his Mississippi, despite its flaws. He expressed optimism about a future where those opposing visions of the state could come together and, once again, a belief in school integration, telling them, "I wish you could have been at the white high school yesterday when I spoke—but the old patterns are crumbling." He closed by expressing his guiding belief in the interconnectedness of the experiences of white and black southerners:

> I can only say, in closing, that we white Southerners and Negro Southerners do indeed have more in common than we have often been given the chance to understand, and that perhaps we should keep this quality in mind in the changing, tumultuous period we are entering. In the meantime, please believe me, for what little it is worth, that this white Yazoo boy's heart is with you.[78]

His fervor for the subject of school desegregation, which compelled him to write *Yazoo*, continued to animate him throughout his career. In 1982, while a visiting faculty member at the University of Mississippi, Morris and his journalism students founded the *Ole Miss Magazine*. He encouraged them to devote a special issue to reflecting upon the legacy of the "Battle of Ole Miss" when two people were killed and dozens were injured in a violent attempt to stave off the token integration of the institution. Allison Brown, the editor of the issue, noted Morris's "inspirational" presence, and the students plunged into what was a continuation of their mentor's work as they documented and tried to understand this painful history.[79]

Thus Morris's belief in the morality and the desirability of meaningful integration was a nearly lifelong passion. During the post-1966 era when many black radicals began loudly to question the desirability of integration as a worthwhile goal, Morris never abandoned his commitment. He did, however, understand the mood of the moment and why some activists had grown weary of ceaselessly facing white hatred and violence and why they would begin to question the desirability of full incorporation into such a dysfunctional world. With a sense of despair, he encapsulated the mood of the day in *Yazoo* when he wrote, "*Integration.* The very word seemed archaic and worn out, a little flighty and frivolous, and the silliest liberals seemed even sillier using it."[80] As a keen observer, although he noticed and understood the mood, he had not imbibed it.

Morris remained a proponent of desegregated schools and wrote *Yazoo* with the optimistic belief that the experiment would work. He was, however, still cognizant of the fact that his desires were not necessarily analogous with those of the black community. He later told an interviewer who asked him, "Do you still believe in desegregation?" that "what I do believe in strongly is *access*, having access to institutions." He acknowledged, "Maybe the blacks don't want it, but given the great sweep of history, let's give them the choice. If they don't want it, fine."[81] The decision about what the partial civil rights revolution would mean to the generation of African Americans who came of age during it was, he realized, not his to make.

When he wrote *Yazoo* he was understandably optimistic about the prospect of a brighter, more racially integrated future. As Morris documented in the book, many community leaders, even some who had previously been members of the white Citizens' Council, came out in support of the public school system, urging white parents not to enroll their children in the private schools that were proliferating throughout the state. Indeed, initially the white attrition rate in Yazoo City was less than expected, and surprisingly some white students who temporarily abandoned the public schools returned after a semester away.[82] In addition to these positive signs, Morris noted much that was negative, including the fact that black administrators were universally demoted during the transition and the significant compromise that although the school buildings themselves were integrated in 1970, individual classrooms initially were not. In the spring of 1970 the United States Justice Department reported that four-fifths of the classes attended by white children in the Yazoo City schools were all or predominately white.[83]

Morris's optimism about the future of school integration may have been in part a product of wishful thinking. Another contemporary observer, Luther Munford, who wrote a precocious senior thesis at Princeton about school desegregation in Mississippi, did not share Morris's rosy assessment. He described a "crazy-quilt" pattern of white leadership in Yazoo City of strong pro-public school forces working in opposition against those who were willing to abandon the school system rather than accept desegregation. While Morris praised Norman Mott, the editor of the *Yazoo City Herald,* for his pro-desegregation editorials and support for the public schools, Munford interpreted him as a symbol of the town's divided consciousness, noting, "Mott took a firm editorial position behind public education but enrolled one of his two school aged children in a private academy; his paper also printed private school press releases verbatim."[84]

Despite its promising start, Morris's hope that meaningful school integration could take place in Yazoo City did not come to fruition. Jim Yardley visited Yazoo City in 1997 to report on the outcome of the city's experiment with integrated education begun more than two and a half decades previously, and what he found was not encouraging. He did, however, discover a seemingly unlikely white proponent of the public school system in the form of Ardis D. Russell, whose father had been the town's notoriously racist police chief while Morris was writing

Yazoo. Russell's daughter Ann graduated from Yazoo City High School in 1997, one of thirty white students in a class of 147. Russell sardonically told Yardley that despite the private Manchester Academy's pretentions to offer a superior education, the town's private school might as well have a sign in front of it reading, *"Manchester: Where Your White Friends Are."*[85] Russell, a 1966 graduate of Yazoo City High School, watched his former school integrate and then witnessed the year-by-year decrease in the number of white students enrolling in the system. This steady attrition is a phenomenon that some attributed to the fact that the pro-integratio n white leadership of the community that Morris praised in *Yazoo* was growing older, dying, and leaving behind a new generation less committed to that goal.[86] Today the public school system is 99 percent black, and most white students attend the Manchester Academy, an institution that Morris once predicted would not have the staying power of the public system.[87]

Later Morris acknowledged that he had "misjudged the efficacy and durability of white private academies in some areas."[88] He also later reflected that he was guilty of "miscalculating though not minimizing the more subtle forms of the old racism just then developing."[89] Finally, he also noted that he had "misjudged, likewise, the corrosive effects of bedrock poverty on the efforts toward enlightened progress."[90] Indeed, although he wrote elsewhere about the fact that many

Mississippians, both black and white, lived in overwhelming poverty, he did not infuse *Yazoo* with a class analysis of that kind, focusing instead on the overwhelming racial divide. A 1967 article from *Look* magazine showed images of an African American family in Yazoo City living in a dilapidated house with no steady income and a food supply that consisted of "flour, a quarter jar of instant coffee and an inch of rice in a cellophane bag."[91] The reporter recounted the story of a local woman who took the drastic step of poisoning her child to spare it from what she feared would be the slower death of starvation.[92] To these individuals, school desegregation was at best a far distant secondary concern.

Despite these self-acknowledged flaws in his analysis, Morris maintained that "in the long sweep of history the event would prove momentous here."[93] Despite the darker aspects of Mississippi's past, he was also convinced that "the Deep South, with all of its failings and complexities, darknesses and bequeathed transgressions, was a symbol and crucible, and had much it could teach the nation."[94] Morris was impatient with northerners who grew too comfortable with a North/South dichotomy, where the South was stigmatized as a racist epicenter and cultural backwater in contrast to a more enlightened North. The region was, he argued in the closing pages of *Yazoo*, "the palliative of the national guilt."[95] The racism that embroiled Mississippi was a national issue.

The New York he writes of was a place of mystery and intellectual stimulation, but it was populated by a fair share of blatant racists and far too many poseurs. Morris was fond of observing the fact that in many ways Mississippi was far more integrated than the allegedly more tolerant and enlightened North.[96] Although his prediction of lasting school desegregation in Yazoo City was incorrect, his belief that the distance between his Mississippi and that that existed in the minds of the 1960s civil rights workers could be minimized or traversed is not without substantiating evidence. In *Yazoo* he noted "among blacks a new commitment to Mississippi *as a place*, expressions of love and loyalty to Mississippi as a society worth working for, as a frontier for redeeming some lost quality in the American soul."[97] He noticed this new attitude in the outlook of an African American refugee who moved from Yazoo City to Chicago but later had the courage to return home, "back to the place where I belong." With that observation, Morris foresaw a reverse migration of African Americans back to the South, a forecast that later became a historical reality.[98]

Today many African Americans who once fled the South's racism and poverty are now returning to it, viewing it as a far more hospitable place than the region they had left. Furthermore, many African Americans who were born in the North but who have southern origins are also relocating south and reclaiming the region that their parents once abandoned in terror or despair. Literally hundreds of thousands of African Americans have moved to the South in the last decade. According to the 2010 census, 57 percent of American black people live in the South, the highest percentage since 1960.[99] Those who make the reverse journey generally find themselves living in a far less segregated environment than they had been in the North.[100] Given the racial violence and repression that many migrants originally fled along with the poverty and lack of opportunities, the fact that so many would return is evidence of a staggering degree of social change of a kind predicted by Morris.

Like all works of great literary merit, *Yazoo* has a timeless quality. It transcends even its deeply significant value as a nuanced and detailed record of a historical moment. The book continues to be relevant, not only because of Morris's powers as a prognosticator who knew that Mississippi was destined to be the site of much racial progress but also because his ruminations on home and displacement and on guilt and longing are universal. Furthermore, *Yazoo*, and indeed much of Morris's writing, stands as an ongoing reminder of the continuing relevance of historical events. The softening of Mississippi's racial divide has been accompanied in some circles by a peculiar historical amnesia about the harsh realities of the past, which have ongoing consequences, particularly in the realm of socioeconomic inequalities.

In 2011 Mississippi governor Haley Barbour, a Yazoo City native, clumsily brought Yazoo City's racial struggles back into the limelight after a profile of him appeared in the conservative magazine the *Weekly Standard.* Perhaps predictably given his privileged position in the community, he had little to say about the struggle for racial equality, recalling simply, "I just don't remember it as being that bad." He also had praise for the Citizens' Council, which he depicted as a force that protected the community from racial violence and sped up the process of integration, rather than as an organization devoted to maintaining segregation by means of a variety of forms of repression. Andrew Ferguson, who wrote the profile, dutifully quoted from *Yazoo.* However, he quoted Morris sparingly and in ways that minimized Morris's angst and seemed to suggest a level of agreement with Barbour's assessment that did not exist. He also downplayed Morris's moral authority by unfairly caricaturing him as "the once-famous Southern overwriter who whipped memories of his Yazoo childhood into a series of sweet, frothy memoirs."[101]

Morris, however, had the last word as historians and other clearer-eyed observers rushed to denounce Barbour's false memories. In the process, Morris's keener observations were resuscitated through the reprinting of more representative excerpts from *Yazoo*.[102] Barbour's fumble makes it clearer than ever how much those who endeavor to understand Mississippi—which Morris saw as a kind of microcosm for the United States—can find no better place to begin than with the writings of Willie Morris, especially *Yazoo: Integration in a Deep-Southern Town.*

JENNIFER JENSEN WALLACH

NOTES

1. Willie Morris, *Yazoo: Integration in a Deep-Southern Town* (New York: Ballantine, 1971), 7.

2. Review of *North Toward Home* by Willie Morris, *Publisher's Weekly*, October 2, 1967; John J. O'Connor, "From a Southerner's Point of View." Review of *North Toward Home* by Willie Morris, *Wall Street Journal*, November 2, 1967. See Jack Bales, *Willie Morris: An Exhaustive Annotated Bibliography and a Biography* (Jefferson, NC: McFarland & Company, 2006) for a truly exhaustive list of writings by and about Willie Morris, including a detailed list of publications that reviewed his various books.

3. Willie Morris, *North Toward Home* (1967; reprint, New York: Dell Publishing, 1967), 141.

4. Willie Morris, *New York Days* (Boston: Little, Brown, & Company, 1993), 9.

5. Morris, *North Toward Home*, 77–78.

6. Lew Powell, "On Being the Famous Writer Willie Morris," *Delta Democrat Times*, May 16, 1971.

7. Morris, *Yazoo*, 8. In a 1980 interview with John Griffin Jones, Morris agreed with this assessment, saying about *Yazoo*, "It's in a way a continuation of *North Toward Home.*" See John Griffin Jones, *Mississippi Writers Talking*, Volume II (Jackson: University Press of Mississippi, 1983), 110.

8. Morris, *New York Days*, 73–74.

9. Larry L. King, *In Search of Willie Morris* (New York: Public Affairs, 2006), 9.

10. Charles C. Bolton, *The Hardest Deal of All: The Battle Over School Integration in Mississippi, 1870–1980* (Jackson: University Press of Mississippi, 2005), 169; Jason Sokol, *There Goes My Everything: White Southerners in the Age of Civil Rights, 1945–1975* (New York: Alfred A. Knopf, 2006), 171; Faustine C. Jones, "Ironies of School Desegregation," *Journal of Negro Education* 47 (1978): 13–15.

11. Morris, *Yazoo*, 10.

12. Neil McMillen, *The Citizens' Council: Organized Resistance to the Second Reconstruction, 1954–64* (Urbana, IL: University of Chicago Press, 1971), 15–40.

13. Willie Morris, *The Ghosts of Medgar Evers: A Tale of Race, Murder, Mississippi, and Hollywood* (New York: Random House, 1998), 42–43; Morris, *North Toward Home*, 177–80; Morris, *Yazoo*, 13–15.

14. Bolton, *The Hardest Deal of All*, 75.

15. Morris, *North Toward Home*, 179–80.

16. Bolton, *The Hardest Deal of All*, 75.

17. McMillen, *The Citizens' Council*, 211.

18. Morris, *The Ghosts of Medgar Evers*, 118.

19. Bolton, *The Hardest Deal of All*, 59; For a further summary of these plans, see McMillen, *The Citizens' Council*, 15–16, and Bolton, *The Hardest Deal of All*, 33–60.

20. For more information about Ivy, see Mississippi Department of Archives and History, Finding Aid for Horace Macaulay Ivy Collection, http://mdah.state.ms.us/manuscripts/z1806.html (accessed July 5, 2011). More details about the relative funding of the black and white

schools systems in 1955 can also be found in H. M. Ivy and Associated Consultants in Education, *Survey of Yazoo City Municipal Separate School District* (Meridian, MS: Associated Consultants in Education, 1995).

21. Morris, *Yazoo*, 13.

22. Lacey McLaughlin, "Integrating Yazoo: Race and Change in Haley Barbour's Hometown," *Jackson Free Press*, March 2, 2011.

23. Willie Morris, "Yazoo . . . notes on survival," T. M. with holograph notes. 71pp, Willie Morris Collection, Archives and Special Collections, J. D. Williams Library, The University of Mississippi, Box 64, Folder 3.

24. Dan Wakefield, "A Time of Pain and Anger, Gentleness and Decency in Mississippi," *New York Times*, May 16, 1971.

25. Fred Hobson, *Tell About the South: The Southern Rage to Explain* (Baton Rouge: Louisiana State University Press, 1983); Morris, *Yazoo*, 10

26. Morris, *North Toward Home*, 90; Morris, *Yazoo*, 145.

27. J. Speed Carroll, "Bright Boy from Yazoo," *New Republic* 157 (1967): 32–24.

28. Morris, *New York Days*, 4.

29. Ibid., 63.

30. Morris, *North Toward Home*, 380.

31. Ibid., 141.

32. For a more extended discussion of this passage, see Jennifer Jensen Wallach, *Closer to the Truth Than Any Fact: Memoir, Memory, and Jim Crow* (Athens: University of Georgia Press, 2008), 99–101, 136.

33. Morris, *The Ghosts of Medgar Evers*, 8.

34. Morris, *Yazoo*, 138.

35. "Yazoo . . . notes on survival," T. M. Photocopy. With holograph notes. 88 pp, Willie Morris Collection, Box 64, Folder 4.

36. Willie Morris, "Yazoo . . . notes on survival," *Harper's*, June 1970, 47.

37. For a lengthier discussion of autobiography, subjectivity, and historical reality, see Wallach, *Closer to the Truth*, 13–35.

38. Morris, *Yazoo*, xi.

39. Ibid., 140.

40. Morris, *North Toward Home*, 30–31.

41. Morris, *Yazoo*, 142.

42. W. E. B. Du Bois, *The Souls of Black Folk* (1903; reprint, New York: Dover Publications, 1994), 2.

43. Although Du Bois's concept of "double consciousness" has particularly racial overtones, Dickson D. Bruce notes that Du Bois drew on a wide variety of intellectual influences when formulating the concept. He may have encountered the term as a description of a psychological state from his Harvard mentor William James. James may have used the term as a medical one, to describe an individual with two distinct personalities. For a longer history of the origin of the phrase, see Dickson D. Bruce, "W. E. B. Du Bois and the Idea of Double Consciousness," *American Literature* 64 (1992): 299–309.

44. Du Bois, *The Souls of Black Folk*, 2.

45. Ibid., 2.

46. Willie Morris, "Coming on Back," in *Shifting Interludes: Selected Essays*, ed. Jack Bales (Jackson: University Press of Mississippi, 2002), 171.

47. Rebecca De Schweinitz, *If We Could Change the World: Young People and America's Long Struggle for Racial Equality* (Chapel Hill: University of North Carolina Press, 2011), 86.

48. Brian Ward, "Forgotten Walls and Master Narratives: Media, Culture, and Memories of the Modern African American Freedom Struggle," in *Media, Culture, and the Modern African American Freedom Struggle*, ed. Brian Ward (Gainesville: University of Florida Press, 2001).

49. Jonathan Yardley, Review of *Yazoo* by Willie Morris, *Greensboro Daily News*, May 9, 1971.

50. James Dickerson, "Willie Morris Comes Home Again to the Delta," reprinted in *Conversations with Willie Morris*, ed. Jack Bales (Jackson: University Press of Mississippi, 2000), 38.

51. Morris, *Yazoo*, 60, 65.

52. Ibid., 47–51.

53. Ibid., 50.

54. Ibid., 49.

55. Accounts of Rudy Shield's activism can be found in Akinyele Omowale Umoja, "'We Will Shoot Back': The Natchez Mode and Paramilitary Organization in the Mississippi Freedom Movement," *Journal of Black Studies* 32, no. 3 (2002): 271–94; Emilye Crosby, editor, *Civil Rights History from the Ground Up* (Athens: University of Georgia Press, 2011); Emilye Crosby, *A Little Taste of Freedom: The Black Freedom Struggle in Claiborne County, Mississippi* (Chapel Hill: University of North Carolina Press, 2005); Emilye Crosby, "'You Got a Right to Defend Yourself': Self-Defense and the Claiborne County, Mississippi Civil Rights Movement," *International Journal of Africana Studies* 9, no. 1 (Spring 2003): 133–64.

56. Crosby, *Civil Rights History from the Ground Up*, 228.

57. Crosby, *A Little Taste of Freedom*, 298

58. Umoja, "'We Will Shoot Back,'" 284.

59. "Committee for Progress Reports on 25 Demands," *Yazoo City Herald*, November 20, 1964.

60. Rudy Shields, "Rudy Shields 'Clears the Air,'" *Yazoo City Herald*, October 9, 1969, 4.

61. "Message for Boycotters" signed "Just a Friend," *Yazoo City Herald*, date unknown, A7, 1969.

62. Marion Morris to Willie Morris, January 14, 1970. Willie Morris Collection, Box 5, Folder 1.

63. William F. Holmes, Review of *Yazoo* by Willie Morris, *Saturday Review*, June 5, 1961.

64. John Griffin Jones, *Mississippi Writers Talking*, Volume II (Jackson: University Press of Mississippi, 1983), 111.

65. Jack Bales, "A Conversation with Willie Morris," in *Conversations with Willie*, ed. Jack Bales (Jackson: University Press of Mississippi, 2000), 158.

66. Clayborne Carson, *In Struggle: SNCC and the Black Awakening* (Cambridge, MA: Harvard University Press, 1981).

67. For a more detailed analysis of some of these interracial tensions, see Emily Stoper, "The Student Nonviolent Coordinating Committee: The Rise and Fall of a Redemptive Organization," *Journal of Black Studies* 8, no. 1 (1977): 24.

68. Willie Morris, "Despair in Mississippi; Hope in Texas," *Dissent* 10 (1963): 220, 226.

69. Morris, *Yazoo*, 114.

70. Morris, *North Toward Home*, 386–87.

71. Morris, *The Ghosts of Medgar Evers*, 12.

72. Morris, *North Toward Home*, 131.

73. Willie Morris, "Best Solution Must Be Slow," *Daily Texan*, December 5, 1954.

74. J. C. Gouldan, "Candidates Want Desegregated UT," *Daily Texan*, April 27, 1955.

75. Willie Morris, "The Round Up," *Daily Texan*, December 20, 1955.

76. Willie Morris, "In a Refreshing Provincial Way," *Texas Observer*, August 15, 1958, 3.

77. Harriet C. DeCell, "Where Is Home for Willie Morris?" *Delta Review*, October 1968, 55.

78. Willie Morris, "Address to the Students of N.D. Taylor School, Yazoo City, MS, April 21, 1967," Willie Morris Collection, Box 107, Folder 1.

79. *The Ole Miss Magazine: The Meredith Crisis in Retrospect, September 30, 1962–September 20, 1982.*

80. Morris, *Yazoo*, 132.

81. Jones, *Mississippi Writers Talking*, 114–15.

82. Luther Munford notes that the white enrollment in the Yazoo City schools actually increased by 11 percent between the spring 1970 and fall 1970 semesters. See Luther Munford, "Black Gravity: Desegregation in 30 Mississippi School Districts" (senior thesis, Woodrow Wilson School, Princeton University, April 16, 1971), 84.

83. Ibid., 121.

84. Ibid., 80.

85. Jim Yardley, "Separate Worlds: A Look into the School Systems of Yazoo City, Mississippi," *Oxford American* 20 (1997): 24.

86. Ibid., 25.

87. McLaughlin, "Integrating Yazoo."

88. Morris, "Coming on Back," 169.

89. Morris, *New York Days*, 336.

90. Ibid., 169.

91. William Hedgepeth, "The Hungry World of Teresa Pilgrim," *Look*, December 26, 1967, 41.

92. Ibid., 44.

93. Morris, "Coming on Back," 169.

94. Morris, *New York Days*, 334.

95. Morris, *Yazoo*, 148.

96. See, for example, Dick Polman, "A Son of the South: Author Willie Morris Speaks Out from the Land He Chronicled in the 60s on Life There in the 80s," in *Conversations with Willie Morris*, ed. Jack Bales, 126. Morris is quoted as saying, "We've had a lot of race problems in Mississippi, and we've got a long way to go, but we're much more integrated than Pennsylvania."

97. Morris, *Yazoo*, 16.

98. Ibid.

99. Larry Copeland, "For Blacks, Return to Southern Roots," *USA Today*, July 1–4, 2011. Morris noted this trend of reverse migration with pleasure in *My Mississippi* (Jackson: University Press of Mississippi, 2000), a book that he collaborated on with his son the photographer David Rae Morris. On p. xiii, he gives some statistics about the reverse migration and exults, "many people of both races were coming home." Morris himself was a reverse migrant.

100. Tom Ashbrook, "African-Americans and the Reverse Migration," On Point Radio Broadcast WBUR Boston, May 28, 2011, http://onpoint.wbur.org/2011/03/28/reverse-migration (accessed July 5, 2011). More information is available at the Schomburg Center for Research in Black Culture, "The African American Migration Experience," http://www.inmotionaame.org/migrations/landing.cfm?migration=11 (accessed July 5, 2011).

101. Andrew Ferguson, "The Boy from Yazoo: Haley Barbour, Mississippi's Favorite Son," December 27, 2010,

http://www.weeklystandard.com/articles/boy-yazoo-city_523551.html?page=1 (accessed July 5, 2011).

102. See, for example, Amanda Terkel, "Jeppie Barbour, Haley's Brother, Bemoaned Blacks 'Not Listen' to Whites Like They Used To,'" December 12, 2010, http://www.huffingtonpost.com/2010/12/20/jeppie-brother-haley-barbour-brother_n_799441.html (accessed July 5, 2011).

YAZOO

Acknowledgments

I want to thank many Mississippians, black and white, for their co-operation and their frankness while I was working on this book. I am also grateful to my colleagues at *Harper's:* Bob Kotlowitz and Midge Decter for their patience while I was away from the office and Herman Gollob of Harper's Magazine Press for his encouragement.

Paul Anthony, Paul Gaston, and their team of reporters at the Southern Regional Council in Atlanta were particularly helpful in sharing their documents and findings. Luther Munford of Jackson, Mississippi, and the Princeton Class of '71 generously allowed me to read his perceptive thesis on Mississippi school integration, *School Reformation.*

As this book went to press, the United States Supreme Court had yet to hand down its crucial decisions on to what extent busing could be used to implement school integration. That decision would have stronger ramifications in the rest of the nation than in the South, but I would have liked for the reaction to it, in Mississippi and elsewhere, to have been part of the narrative.

This volume by no means pretends to be a "definitive" study of my native state during the year following massive racial integration of its first school districts. Rather it is one writer's very personal view, supported by a considerable amount of talking and moving about, of the important events which took place there in 1969 and 1970.

W. M.

Two huge American minorities have so far largely eluded the great assimilation. They are, ironically, the oldest and (barring the redskins only) the most indigenously American minorities of all. Both of them were established here before the Pilgrims hit Plymouth Rock. They are the oldest and the most durable of the "hyphenates"—the Southern-Americans and their ancient contemporaries, the Negro-Americans. . . . It is, in fact, impossible to imagine one without the other and quite futile to try.

—C. Vann Woodward

The tendency to romanticise school desegregation in the South grows daily. The talismans we white southerners hand round to keep our spirits up, to explain what the hell we're doing with our lives, to encourage waverers or just to pass the time of day are finding their way into the national outlook.

Integration is taking place under the gun in Mississippi. The people who have fought it since 1954 have lost in the courts but are still fighting it in all the other ways at their disposal. They are still the school-boards: they delay, obstruct, fake, cheat wherever they can.

Who is surprised? We still have people firmly believing if we go through the minimum motions, do not call attention to ourselves, this madness will pass and we can go back to our own way of life. Haven't we always deluded ourselves endlessly?

Our magic amulet: if left alone the kids will work it out together. The kids aren't going to be left alone to work it out and without some positive assistance, some powerful, dramatic, civilizing leadership you know the country needs, we will etch our racism so indelibly there will never be any hope for us.

—*Letter to the author from a white liberal in Mississippi, January 14, 1971*

PART ONE

1

November, 1969

The last time I had been there, I had gone to see my grandmother, whom I call Mamie. She is ninety-five years old, the youngest of sixteen children and the only one of them still alive. My mother, who lives alone with her now, telephoned me in New York to say that Mamie had just had a stroke and I should come right away; it might be my last time to see her.

Her great-great-uncle had been the first territorial governor of Mississippi, before it was admitted to the Union, and her people had settled the state when it was still called "the Southwest." Another uncle had been the United States senator through the 1840s, had given the dedication address at the Washington Monument, and had defeated his blood enemy Jefferson Davis for governor in 1851; all over the South before the final break, he defended "the good old Union, the fruit of the sage counsels of our immortal ancestors." Her father had been a Confederate major and a newspaper editor; an obscure and unidentified Federal captain, under direct orders from Sherman, had deposited his printing presses in a well when his troops marched through his little town, Raymond, on the way to Jackson, which was considerably larger game. She was born not long after the Federal soldiers pulled out of Mississippi. In the old family burial plot, the only recognizable grave now is her eldest brother's; she must be one of the few living people with a sibling who was born in 1851.

Time weaves its small eccentric ironies on us, its children. Are we really much removed from then? A great-uncle of William Styron, my Virginia friend now living in the East, was the state treasurer when my great-uncle was governor. My great-grandfather was a leader of the Mississippi legislative committee that impeached the Republican Reconstructionist governor, a proper New Englander named Adelbert Ames, the great-grandfather of my friend George Plimpton.

Now Mamie lies in the back room of the house where I grew up in Yazoo. She is completely blind and almost completely deaf. Some of the time she is with us here in the present, as lucid and full of good humors as she was when I was a boy and loved her more deeply than I loved anyone else; but mostly she inhabits an old woman's whirling misty shadows and premonitions, mistaking me for her brother Samuel Dawson Harper, who has been dead sixty years, talking with the spirits of her vanished sisters when they were children in Raymond, asking my grandfather Percy if he wants his chicken fried or broiled for supper in the tiny brick house across from the Jitney Jungle on North Jefferson Street in Jackson. Sometimes she thinks my son David is me.

I have brought David with me on this trip. I want him to have the chance to remember her. He is a New York City boy. He is ten years old, and he has been riding the subways alone for three years, loving the noise and speed of those subterranean phenomena which for his father are only dark and brutal monstrosities. Occasionally he makes fun of my Southern accent, though he asks me more and more as he gets older about where his people came from. For a present three years ago, he typed away secretly for two days on my typewriter and later came out with a framed copy of the Gettysburg Address, done with his own fine Yankee hand. It had its share of typos, and it began, "Dear Daddy—The Gettyburg: Four score and seeven year ago . . ." and concluded, "The Ent— Love, David." I took him to Gettysburg after that, showing him Cemetery Ridge, Big Round Top and Little Round Top, the Wheat Field, Seminary Ridge, and the rounded green valley where on the afternoon of July 3, 1863, the idea that we were to become, after all, a mass multiracial democracy may have been decided, among American boys tearing each other to death with canister, bayonets, rifle butts, and big old stones. He wanted a present for himself, and when I took him into a store close to where Longstreet had set up his artillery, he decided, among all the modern artifacts of what happened there, on a gray infantry hat. While I was paying the clerk, $1.75 plus three cents Pennsylvania sales tax, I noticed he was pondering the gray hat, finally putting it back in place and taking a blue one instead, which he calmly put on his head. When we got in the car, I said nothing for a few minutes. The road we were driving traced the line of Lee's great retreat, and the sun's late-summer glow caught the monuments and the cannon in the splendid battlefield tableau that fills every Southern boy's heart with a wonderful dread and excitement. Finally I said, "Why did you pick the blue hat instead of the gray one?" He replied, "Because I don't want to be nobody's slave."

We had driven now the forty-eight miles from Jackson in a rented car, across the hills in autumn with their dead kudzu, and we reached the town after dark. I had timed it deliberately, because we were leaving again the next morning, and for several quite good reasons I did not want anyone to know I was home. My mother was there, and Mamie sat up in the bed and reached out to embrace us. I had forgotten my own fears as a child of sick old people, fears of their smells, of their tenacity and irascible durability, and the boy went away for a while, to look at the various mementos in my old room, the trinkets and souvenirs of my small-town pubescence. Viola was there too—the Negro woman almost as old as my grandmother, frail and very gray now but still quite healthy, who had worked for the family for more than a generation, had slept and lived in the house during its times of crisis, who had come to know us in our several disasters of the flesh, and who now sat in a chair several hours every day next to the bed. She was a sturdy physical presence in this place of decay, and even though three others of us were here in the room with her, Mamie would extend her hand every so often, stretch out her entire gnarled and skinny old arm, and cry, *"Viola! Viola! Where's Viola?"* "I'm right here, honey," Viola would say, taking her hand and stroking it, carrying on a steady torrential half-monologue all the while. This scene, my mother said to me, took place all day long. A few days later, at a fine sophisticated dinner party given by friends on the Upper East Side, I described what I had seen. A well-known New York writer said, "That's the most racist description I've ever heard." And the writer's wife added, "It's a racist description of a corrupt and racist society."

2

January, 1970

My grandmother had survived the stroke, and this time, in January and later in March, I went back to Yazoo for different reasons. The United States Supreme Court had ordered thirty school districts in Mississippi* to completely integrate their schools immediately—a harbinger, sixteen years after the *Brown* decision, for the rest of the South and, presumably, the nation. Compliance with the latest Supreme Court decision, or even a substantial degree of compliance, meant, as any Southerner would tell you, the beginnings of a true revolution, revolution of a kind that had not so much as touched the South, not to mention other Americans. Yazoo, sitting incongruously on the edge of the great delta, half white and

---

*Under *Alexander v. Holmes,* October 28, 1969, the existence of any all-black school in a school district was proof that the old dual system was still in effect. The "all deliberate speed" of the 1954 *Brown* decision was no longer permissible.

half black, was one of the thirty districts.

I did not want to go back. I conjured many elaborate reasons, a dozen dramatic interior motives, for avoiding it. At least five times I promised myself, firmly and irrevocably, that I would not go. My office friends will testify to these curious emotional gyrations, these jolting peregrinations of a vainglorious heart, which tormented me relentlessly during a grim wintry Manhattan fortnight. *I did not want to go.* I had written a book a couple of years before, *North Toward Home,* which was about myself and about the people I had grown up among in Yazoo, and except for the one brief secret nocturnal visit, I had not been back since. My book, as such things always do in our country, had deeply disturbed the town. Many people there thought I had damaged and condemned it. One person wrote me that I had besmirched the memory of my father.* Another wrote a letter published on the front page of the Yazoo *Herald* that I had embarrassed my church, my school, and my friends. My mother received a few threatening calls. I got pointed warnings about what would happen if I ever came back. Since Yazoo did not have a bookstore, the publishers had placed a substantial number of copies in

---

*In fact, the gentleman who wrote me this had been encouraged to leave town quite a few years before for taking off his trousers, in the most flourishing manner, in front of a little girl, so now he was living elsewhere. I wrote him back: "Dear———, I profoundly disagree that I besmirched the memory of my father, but you certainly did your damnedest to besmirch ——— ———."

the P & S Pharmacy on Main Street, which had sold out in short order. My old friend Bubba Barrier, my best friend since we were three years old, who now helps run his father Hibbie's plantation, telephoned me long distance in New York. Bubba said, "I just want you to know one thing. This book of yours is the biggest thing to hit town since the Civil War." You couldn't walk twenty feet, Bubba said, without hearing an earnest conversation about it. People were standing in line to get it at the library. "I think half the people in town kind of likes it," Bubba said, "and may be a little proud of it. The other half of the town is extremely agitated." Bubba went on to say he had the impression that the half which was so agitated consisted mainly of the people who were not in the book.

After a while, I believe, this reaction, which amazed, baffled, and for a time deeply disturbed me, though I of all people should have appreciated its origins, softened considerably. This too is a very American phenomenon. For a number of people there—Bubba, and my old English teacher Mrs. Parker, and the editor of the paper, and the librarian, and especially the good old boys with whom I grew up, some now scattered all over the South (Henjie Henick, Muttonhead Shepherd, Ralph Atkinson, Big Boy Wilkinson, Peewee Baskin, Honest Ed Upton, Van Jon Ward, Robert Pugh, Billy Rhodes, Moose Moorhead, *good ole Mississippi boys*)—realized, I believe, that my book had been written as an act of love; sensed, perhaps, Faulkner's understanding that one loves a place not just because of but despite.

Yet all this was not my only excuse. The most terrible burden of the writer, the common burden that makes writers a fraternity in blood despite their seasonal expressions of malice, jealousy, antagonism, suspicion, rage, venom, perfidy, competition over the size of publishers' advances—that common burden is the burden of memory. It is an awesome weight, and if one isn't careful it can sometimes drive you quite mad. It comes during moments when one is half asleep, or after a reverie in the middle of the day, or in the stark waking hours: a remembrance of everything in the most acute detail from one's past, together with a fine sense of the nuances of old happenings and the most painful reconsideration of old mistakes, cruelties, embarrassments, and sufferings, and all this embroidered and buttressed by one of the deepest of urges, the urge to dramatize to yourself about yourself, which is the beginning of at least part of the urge to create. Since my town is the place which shaped me, for better or worse, into the creature I now am, since it nurtured me and gave me much of whatever sensibility I now possess, since it is a small Deep-Southern place where the land and the remembered places have changed very little, where the generations come and go in the context of these common and remembered places and amidst the same drawn-out seasons, where mortality itself grips and maddens one's consciousness in the missing faces, in all the children who have grown up toward middle age and all the middle-aged adults who dominated your boyhood and are now terribly, painfully old—I knew, as I had known for some time, that going back for me, even more than exposing myself in some new notoriety, would bring the most intense emotional pain.

Given all these circumstances, one should not be surprised to hear that a premonition had been working its way up my frontal lobe; at first it was a mere grain of sand, but eventually it grew to enormous proportions. This premonition was that I would meet there, on my home ground, a violent death, perhaps even a death accompanied by mutilation and unfathomable horror. My premonition had an animal force to it, unlike all the other premonitions in my life. *Some bastard is going to kill me in Yazoo.* Although I may not be one's paradigm of heroic courage, I am not easily frightened, having indeed sometimes courted danger, and as a somewhat harried editor working in the state of Texas, found myself often in situations full of potential violence, danger, and mayhem. I know a great deal more about violence, say, than the perfervid nihilists and pop-art guerrilla fighters of the New Left, on Manhattan Island and elsewhere, who were all for it as the prevailing fashion—confrontation tactics, some call it—and who had yet to dwell for any considerable time in certain places in America where if you talk violence with any consistency, you are sure to get it in whatever form you want it to come at you. Yet there was no avoiding that I had this on my mind, and it provided another among the several highly valid excuses to remain right here on safe, sane Manhattan Island. I finally went home because the urge to be there during Yazoo's most critical moment was too elemental to resist, and because I would have been ashamed of myself if I had not.

3

One can only imagine what slavery was like in the delta land around Yazoo City—the black alluvial soil, once the very floor under the sea, which had to be fought through all the seasons and elements, reclaimed from the swamps in unbearable summer heat and against the overflowing snake-infested rivers and creeks in the spring: "... this land which man has deswamped and denuded and derivered in two generations...." It was a land that was not easy to defeat, and no one has chronicled this better than Faulkner, who lived eighty miles up the road from here but knew very well this dreadful curse on the land itself, the price it exacted in the sweat and suffering of men, especially in the wild black chattel whose descendants, here in Yazoo and other delta towns six generations later, would soon be going en masse into the schools built by white men for their white children, under the dictates of a supreme federal authority hundreds of miles away. "That's the one trouble with this country," Faulkner says in *As I Lay Dying.* "Everything, weather, all, hangs on too long. Like our rivers, our land: opaque, slow, violent; shaping and creating the life of man in its implacable and brooding image."

The very name *Yazoo* had been an effective and peculiarly haunting subject for speculation among Northern journalists who had visited here frequently of late; Yazoo means "death" or "waters of the dead," and the occasional SNCC worker who came here and then left quickly in the early 1960s when the Movement was in full flower, who called Yazoo County one of the "toughest" in all of Mississippi, knew about the word too. The Northern visitor is invariably surprised when he comes to my home town to find it is not the raw little hill town that the name may deserve —not a Canton, say, or a Philadelphia in Neshoba County—but a substantial town with many broad old streets and beautiful homes peopled by an extremely large number of college-educated whites for this section of the country. The trees and the vegetation are lush and green most of the year; in springtime there is no more beautiful place in America. The smell of the spring is staggering, enveloping the senses, making them reel in pleasurable delight. One writer from New York, emerging from a car here one April night years ago, said, "What's that I smell—a chocolate factory?" The population of the town in 1970 was about 11,000, slightly more than 50 per cent Negro, and in a county of just over 27,000 there are fewer than 2,000 industrial jobs. Almost one-fourth of the population received food stamps, and 35 per cent of the families made less than $3,000 a year. In national elections it is a deeply conservative place. It voted for Goldwater in '64, and for Wallace in '68, and its conservatism is of a piece with the conservatism of the delta as a whole. There is a story that made the rounds during the days of the Movement about the Negro sharecropper, named Ben McGee, who died at the age of seventy-five, ascended to heaven, and was immediately escorted into the presence of the Lord.

"Ben McGee," the Lord said, embracing him in an L.B.J.-like hug, "I'm proud of you. We've kept our eyes on you. Richard Goodwin had been helping us keep tabs on you. You've done the cause of human brotherhood and Christianity so much good down in the Mississippi delta that we intend to send you back."

"O Lord," Ben McGee said. "I'm not going back. You've never been. You don't know what it's like down there."

"If necessary, Ben," the Lord said, "I'm going to have to put that in the form of an order."

"If you send me back down to the delta, Lord," Ben asked, "will you go with me?"

"I'll go as far as Memphis," the Lord replied.

As late as 1948, in Yazoo County, there were more than eighty schools for Negroes. This was the year that Mississippi began underwriting a few tentative efforts to make the schools for Negroes at least reasonably passable, since its leaders after the Dixiecrat split began to fear the possibility of some kind of federal encroachment. Most of these eighty-odd schools in Yazoo County, as one can only guess, were one-room shacks on plantations and in the hills, with one teacher for all the grades and with little more than a rudely transient student population because of the cotton picking in the fall and the chopping in the spring. There were no school buses for Negroes, no indoor plumbing, and no central heating. In 1966, twelve years after the *Brown* decision, the Department of Health, Education, and Welfare cut off federal funds from the Yazoo City schools for their failure to comply with federal guidelines on token "freedom-of-choice" integration. The first black children came into the white schools in 1967, and by September of 1969, before the Court order on full-scale integration went out, there were fewer than one hundred Negroes in white schools out of a total school enrollment in the town of more than 3,500. Even this small black enrollment did not take place without the usual agonies of the soul and dark rages against the federal power.

Fifteen years before, in 1955, in the summer before my senior year at the University of Texas, I came home shortly after the national NAACP had circulated a petition in Yazoo City advocating integration of the schools. The local white Citizens Council was set up then to deal with this problem, and I went to their organizational meeting in the school auditorium. The Council went to work to coerce fifty-three of the Negroes who signed the petition to withdraw their names, and the methods used were not very pretty and did little for the dignity and honor of the town. "Give an inch and they take a mile," was the clarion. White employers immediately fired the signers of the petition who worked for them. Those petitioners who rented houses were evicted by their landlords. White grocers refused to sell food to any of them. Negro grocers who had signed the petition no longer got any groceries from the wholesale stores. After several weeks, all the names had been withdrawn, and a number of Negroes who had been there all their lives were forced into leaving town altogether. Later that year, I was invited to give a speech at the luncheon meeting of the Rotary Club, freshly graduated and on my way to school in England with a Texas diploma, and I told the Rotarians I didn't necessarily agree personally with what I was about to suggest, but they could at least take a lesson from the British conservatives and surrender some part of what they cherished—namely, complete racial segregation—for the sake of preserving the broad essentials of the society they wanted to keep. They should integrate their schools right away, I said, not just tokenly, either; educate the whole white community to the necessity and the decency of this; become a model for the entire state of Mississippi and, indeed, a symbol for the nation. Otherwise they would have a revolution in Yazoo someday and it most decidedly would not be of their own making; perhaps it was their responsibility to prepare the people of Yazoo in civilized and humane ways for the inevitable. Afterward two or three of the leaders came up to me trembling in rage, saying they didn't know what I was talking about and that I was advocating heresy if not bloodshed.

What had happened there in the fifteen years since the Citizens Council forced the fifty-three Negroes to take their names off a petition was similar to what happened throughout the state. There were a few weak glimmers of a new awareness, the stirring of the blacks under the example of Martin Luther King, the faith among them in the ideal of a truly just and integrated society, the gradual halting movement of the whole federal authority through the courts, through Kennedy and Johnson and voting-rights laws toward some dramatic thrust. But by and large among the whites the failure of leadership, symbolized in the Meredith fiasco at Ole Miss in 1962 and the violence of the '64 summer, was so profound as to border on the tragic. Intelligent white Mississippians became so embroiled in sophistical legalisms that the real human issue passed them by altogether. Everywhere there was, as Pat Watters has written, "the possessive old men who held an iron grip on churches, culture centers, and other establishments in which racism was not too apparently a factor in policies." In reaction, and principally in desperation, black leaders in Mississippi, and in Yazoo, were turning at last to a semblance of black-power rhetoric; they were becoming tougher and more sophisticated in their techniques. In early 1964, there was not a single Negro child in an integrated school in Mississippi. One hundred Negro children entered the first grade of white schools in Jackson in September of that year. Throughout much of the period from 1954 to now, the whites in Yazoo, as in so many areas of the Deep South, excluded the Negroes from any remotely significant access to power and abused their own white moderates. "As ye sow," a black leader in town would say to me, "so shall ye reap."

In 1970 in Yazoo, I would find, the demoralized NAACP of 1955 had given way to a strong and active membership of several hundred, with a leadership that was not ashamed of its associations with the organization considered Uncle-Tom in the North. The Yazoo chapter had organized an effective economic boycott of white stores that was now several months old, and had forced several businesses to close. I would see among blacks a new commitment to Mississippi *as a place,* expressions of a love and loyalty to Mississippi as a society worth working for, as a frontier for redeeming some lost quality in the

American soul. "I came back to a place where I belong," one of the blacks in Yazoo who had returned from Chicago would tell me. "If I'm gonna fight for what I believe in, I want to fight for it at home." Fifteen years is either a long time or a short time in the troublesome activities of the human race; it depends on who you are and where you have been. The night before I flew home, back in January, Fannie Lou Hamer was on NBC television, speaking to a large group of Negro children about to go into the white school in a town just north of Yazoo. "You not just *frightened,* you scared to death, ain't you? *You scared to death.* But you jus' remember, they ain't gonna be savin' *you.* You gonna be savin' *them.* "

4

The town has changed remarkably little in twenty years, and as I drive these streets which are a map on my consciousness, I see the familiar places—the hills and trees and houses—in a strange, dreamlike quality, as if what I am seeing here is not truly real, but faintly blurred images caught in my imagination from a more pristine time. I see people walking on the sidewalks on Main Street or Broadway or Grand Avenue who should have been dead long ago, unexpected wisps from the past, but their names come back right away, and with the names the recognition of encounters, conversations, fragments of experience from a quarter of a century ago.

Main Street on this cold and wistfully mournful January day is all but deserted, the result, people tell me, of the Negroes' boycott. Tommy Norman's Drug Store, across from the Taylor & Roberts Feed & Seed Store and Radio Station WAZF, is boarded up and dead; a generation ago, on Saturdays, great crowds of Negroes would have been in front of Tommy's, and inside, along a long wooden counter, whites and blacks, segregated on each side, would have drunk their beer or Nehi strawberry, face-to-face and juxtaposed. On Saturday nights, when we were in high school, we would have taken our girls to the midnight show at either the Palace or the Dixie, finding out in advance which one our friends had chosen so we could all go together. The Palace is now a burnt-out hull, and the Dixie, at Broadway and Main, has vanished from the face of the earth; most of the boys and girls who ate popcorn and held hands and wished the show would finish so they could go park and rub up together on Brickyard Hill, have long since departed for other places. Only the Yazoo Theater, over on Washington Street, remains; it is showing an Elvis Presley picture, *Change of Habit.* Several cars parked in front, next to the building which quarters the Chamber of Commerce, have bumper stickers which say, "YAZOO'S ALIVE AND DOING WELL."

The lumberyard and paint store on Canal, across from the Confederate monument, still displays the big sign, "VISIT OUR COLOR BAR." Behind it, in the colored section, a white postman has put his mailbag on the ground near a house and is playing cards with three Negroes. Further down Main, I see a tall, thin man wearing glasses shuffling along in front of the furniture store. I know the walk, and from fifty yards away, out of the instinct of recognition, I see it is my old companion Henjie Henick, who runs the tire store. "People here are complaining about what you wrote," he once said in a letter to me. "I tell them, everything he says happened, and it happened just like he said it did." I haven't seen Henjie in fifteen years, but I do not stop now to say hello. At the Yazoo Motel earlier that day, the lady behind the counter had said, when I checked in, "I haven't seen you since you were this big," extended an arm, waving it downward about ten inches from the floor. "I wouldn't have recognized you. Why, you're a grown man!" with a look of exasperation and despair.

I drove by my old high school, where the next morning the white students would be joined and outnumbered by the Negro high school students coming in a group from their school. It was as pleasant and settled at the end of the broad avenue as it was eighteen years before; the inscription on the entrance said, "Education—Knowledge" over the statue of Plato holding a book, and the plaque bearing the Ten Commandments was there, as it had always been. Here, in front of this entrance, we once waited for the bell to ring, sitting in small groups on the grass on warm spring mornings, enjoying the pleasant, driftless Southern life, talking parties and baseball and school spirit, and giving hardly a mind to our colored contemporaries who went to "Yazoo High Number 2" on the other side of town; giving little thought to the "separate-but-equal" *modus vivendi* under which, in the early 1950s, the sovereign state of Mississippi was providing us with our education. We were sheltered, I suppose, from much of the humanity around us, privileged white benefactors of our honored and acknowledged Mississippi way of life, and we grew to love the town and the school as our departing came nearer. The school ground is empty on this day, and I have three companions I am showing the town to— two New Yorkers and an editor from Alabama—and they remark on the loveliness of my old schoolhouse. I would like to show them the good old boys lazing there in the yard, and the soft-skinned, double-named belles who shared those days: Daisye Love and Werdna Dee and Libby Terrell and Nettie Taylor and Barbara Nell and Ina Rae, and all the others who should be sitting here, precisely where I left them in May of 1952. I have taken my friends all over town, showing them the houses surrounded by magnolias and elms and locusts, and also the lean-tos and shacks with stilts on the dirt roads of the colored section. The Alabama editor complains that I have not shown him the jailhouse, but the dark has set in, and he says, knowing the South as well as I, "It's a good ole town."

I had a wife, a Texas girl, who hated this place, hated the town and its people with a terrible and disparaging contempt. She believed it elementally evil. She hated everything about Mississippi, and once she wrote a graduate school treatise calling William Faulkner a second-rater. I believe her contempt sprang largely from the fear which often works on outsiders when they come here, fear among other things of its extraordinary apposition of violence and gentleness. For her, Mississippi was a symbol of all that was wrong with all of us, so that even what it inspired in the way of literary sensibility was, to any sound and secure academic mind, also an aberration. On the night Martin Luther King was killed in Memphis, as forlorn and grief-laden a night as I have ever lived, she slapped me across the face and said, *"You Southern boys have a lot to be guilty about."*

There are those who say New York City is a provincial enclave, and that it is unrepresentative of the rest of the nation. I have lived on Manhattan Island eight years now, and for the first two or three in the Big Cave, in the dreadful hardening of one's senses for survival in the cultural capital, I shared in many of these fears. But gradually I grew to feel that New York, far from being an estuary of our national life, is if anything more *representative* than not, more American than otherwise, precisely because it brings together the whole range and spectrum, manifestation and extreme, of the American temperament, of the American races, of all our ways of living and our ways of speaking. New York has become to me the crux and apogee of our contemporary experience, and yet it drives me back almost against the will toward my past. Growing up in a small isolated town of the Deep South a generation ago, I became aware of the life of that place as a cross section and a microcosm of my time and region, and much that was typical of humanity was there for me to judge and to comprehend. What I missed a generation ago were the great exertions of the national presence, the manifestations of the relentless movement toward homogeneity and nationalization—the farthest nerve endings of Americans as a civilization—toward some kind of accommodation, however fragile and illusory this would seem, among our races and peoples and our separate collective pasts. This generation of children, white and black, in Yazoo will not, I sense, be so isolated as mine, for they will be confronted quite early with the things it took me years to learn, or that I have not learned at all.

5

The Fifth Circuit Court of Appeals, which of all the federal appellate courts has been the most active in implementing the racial decisions of the United States Supreme Court, gave the Yazoo schools, after a series of delays, until January 7, 1970, to comply with the law of the land. The law of the land now meant, as it pertained to Yazoo and the thirty Mississippi districts, complete school integration. The guidelines established by the Department of Health, Education, and Welfare would be followed in Yazoo City: the white high school would be the high school for the entire town, with the Negro students coming over en masse from their high school. The Negro high school would become the junior high school for the town; the white junior high students would move in a bloc to that building. Four other schools, including the previously all-black elementary school, would be integrated according to a racial pairing by grades. If every white student in town remained in the public schools, the high school under the HEW plan would be 42 per cent black, the junior high roughly 50 per cent black, and the various grade schools somewhere between 55 and 70 per cent black.

Since the October Supreme Court mandate, the white community in Yazoo had been undergoing an agony of survival. The Nixon Administration, with which that community sympathized, had tried to slow the pace of integration, but its deliberate conservatism had not prevented the Court from acting on its own. Many intelligent, well-meaning whites were baffled and perplexed. "We see on television that the Negro militants say integration doesn't matter any more," one of them said to me. "We hear the Administration doesn't believe in it, either. Does it or doesn't it matter? We're acting on the assumption down here that it does. We're trying to believe in it. Are we right or wrong?" Because there would be, under any circumstances, an exodus of white students to the private school which was already in operation in the white Methodist, Presbyterian, and Baptist churches, a predominantly black public school system was inevitable. The important question, as the January 7 deadline approached, was just how many white children would remain in the public schools, and with what consequences. Yazoo, and other places like it, was getting no inspiration from the President of the United States himself, and what they desperately needed at this juncture was some kind of effective inspiration.

The town was alive with rumors and speculations. A number of whites predicted violence, and the great majority expected the public schools to collapse under the black presence. The private school was openly courting the disaffected whites. A prominent lawyer prophesied that not a single white child would turn up in any of the previously all-black schools on the appointed day. Criticism of the Supreme Court was as intense and pointed as ever; it was as if that leviathan had had a bad night, and woke up the next morning and said before breakfast, "We're going to do something today about Mississippi." Yet this time there was a difference. Even the most diehard white saw an inevitability now, and sensed that after sixteen years of legal delays, the blacks were indeed going to go into the white schools whether their children stayed with those schools or not. The full weight of our history, forged in bloodshed and laws and expressions of ideals, was about to fall on Yazoo, and the people knew it.

A leader of the local VFW wrote the Yazoo *Herald* late in December, in reference to Negro leadership, the boycott, and the integration of the schools: "To the many fine, colored people I can only say this: you are a part of our community, you have helped to raise our children, worked in our homes, but you have deserted us. You have left us to follow the outsiders who came here. They take your hard-earned money, tell you where to go, what to do, with whom to talk. And when

you can give no more, they will leave you here. . . .
May I suggest that you return to the churches you left,
and kneel down and ask the good Lord's help. Then
ask your troublemakers to go somewhere else, to let
you live as you know you must." A white woman told
me, "If I had a child, I'd go out and collect empty
bottles if necessary to send him to private school."
Another woman, describing the "sassy niggers" who
used foul language and were unable to write a simple
sentence, predicted that they would destroy the whole
town and then celebrate its destruction. My mother,
who teaches music in our house on Grand Avenue,
had promised to drive every day at lunchtime to the
junior high school, which is in the colored section
and, as such things go in small Southern towns, a
block from her house, to pick up two little white girls
for their lessons so they wouldn't have to walk the few
hundred yards through dangerous territory. Just
before the opening day, the Negro teachers who
would remain in the previously all-black junior high
school organized a reception for the white parents
who would be sending their children there. One
white mother remarked to one of her acquaintances,
who was sending her children to private school,
"Why, everything was so clean, it smelt good, and
they had electric typewriters and everything." And
her friend replied, "Well, what do you expect? All the
niggers were in the building the day before, sprayin'
and scrubbin' with every sweet-smellin' thing they

could get their hands on." Another white mother who went to the same reception came back and said a Negro teacher had introduced herself to her. "What do you teach?" the·white mother asked, and she said the Negro teacher replied, *"I teaches English."*

6

Yet elsewhere, all over town, there were suggestions that something new was coming to the surface here, something never quite articulated with any degree of force or with the courage of numbers in many Deep-Southern towns, some painful summoning from deepest wellsprings. There were whites in town who fully intended to keep their children in the public schools, and who not only would say so openly, but who after a time would even go further and defend the very notion itself of integrated education as a positive encouragement to their children's learning. At first this spirit was imperceptible, but gradually, under the influence of some of Yazoo's white leaders and with the emergence of others of like mind, it became a movement with noticeable strength behind it. The economic health of the town, its attractiveness to outside industry, was the most consistent argument of the pro-public-school whites, but buttressing this, in the most unexpected places, were feelings infinitely more subtle and significant. There was the white Baptist preacher who said he could not live with himself if he did not keep his child in the public school; the white businessman who said he thought his son should be educated with as many different kinds of children as possible to prepare himself for "real life"; the white mother who said the two races must learn to live with each other or all of Mississippi would never amount to much of anything; the white Catholic nun who wrote to the newspaper that if white and black children—especially between the ages of kindergarten and junior high—"are not brought together in some way in this country, this state, this city, America will inevitably face deeper problems"; the white father who said he would not send his children to private school because the private school was based less on education than on "pure ole hate"; the white teacher who quoted Tocqueville and said the diversity of American experience demanded the need for integrated schooling; the white lawyer who said the South could show the North a thing or two about whites and blacks getting along together. For their part, the black leaders were encouraging the Negro students to make friends if possible, to make the best of a difficult situation if necessary. The confusion was not all on the white side. Some black parents were concerned too. There were to be uprootings of black children as well as white children, and this meant new transportation problems, disruption of school organizations, separation of classmates, and a new existence for many blacks.*

Setting the tone for the white moderates was the Yazoo *Herald,* the weekly newspaper. When I was growing up, I started writing sports for the *Herald* when I was twelve, using a strange argot that must have been incomprehensible to the occasional dirt farmer who might have followed my white-hot dispatches from the playing fields of Eden, Satartia, Flora, and Bentonia. The *Herald*'s editorial tone had changed considerably since those halcyon Dixiecrat days. Beginning with the October Supreme Court decision, the *Herald* took a firm position behind the public schools, and became one of several forces of rationality in the community. "Yazoo City has been fortunate in many crises," one of its editorials said last fall, "because we seem to have a reservoir of enlightened readers (both black and white) willing to persevere through adversity and do what's right. We urge you all, our readers, to rise to the challenge of the transition being required of us. Certainly there will be perplexities and problems of human misunderstanding, but also opportunities and inspirations to all children of this community and their future."

The editors of the student newspaper in the white high school, the *Yazooan,* followed this example. In

*W. F. Minor, *New South* (Winter 1970).

October, they editorialized: "Without a public school system a democratic society cannot exist. If a society limits the basic principle of equal opportunity by limiting the education which is available, it has become oligarchical and not democratic in nature. We of the *Yazooan* staff believe that Mississippi must give total support to the public school system as the best possible means of education for everyone." In December, three weeks before the deadline, the white students wrote:

YHS faces massive integration for the first time next semester. We feel that all students who have begun school this year in the public schools should continue in them next semester because they will be receiving the best education available. The quality of education may even increase with the addition of students and teachers and the new influx of ideas. At the very least, whatever temporary inconveniences are created by overcrowdedness can be alleviated by the advantages of a better education in an accredited school for black students and the opportunity for white students to learn to handle racial problems more successfully than they have been handled in the past. Certainly we cannot even begin to attack the problems that surround us by running away from them, or ignoring them.

On the whole it was pragmatic economics, however, which was playing the leading role. Owen Cooper, the most powerful man in town as president of the Mississippi Chemical Corporation and one of the state's leading Baptists, was a quiet and effective influence. "Owen was almost alone among white establishment figures in Mississippi. He woke up one day a few years ago and all of a sudden realized blacks and whites have to live together," an editor from a delta town said to me. "He wants Yazoo to survive. With him it's a combination of good religion and good business." In the weeks leading to the school deadline, there was never any formal organization of the white moderates. Rather they were operating under what one leader called a "loose confederation" with several key members of the Chamber of Commerce, stressing the expense involved in sending a child to private school and the impossibility of establishing decent private facilities overnight.

On the night of November 24, "one of the largest crowds ever to gather in Yazoo City," as the *Herald* described it, and certainly the first integrated audience to meet "indoors," crowded into the high school auditorium—some one thousand whites and two hundred Negroes—to uphold the public schools. Twenty-five white leaders spoke, including the state senator, the state representative, all the school officials, businessmen, lawyers, coaches, and parents. A white Methodist preacher sought "divine help in removing hatreds, prejudices, and jealousies," and a white Baptist preacher prayed that people "won't abandon the legacy of the past, but instead provide for our children and our children's children." All this was considerably removed from the Citizens Council meeting I sat in on fifteen years before, when massive school integration had the support of fifty-three Negro names on a petition.

This mass meeting might have been the most dramatic espousal of integrated public schools in the history of Mississippi, and perhaps of the Deep South. Yet all through December, and into the first week of January, many advocates of the segregationist private schools scoffed at the notion that any substantial number of white children would tolerate wholesale mingling with blacks, and even among the white moderates there was a guarded pessimism. His Honor the Mayor of Yazoo expected violence. A white teacher told me the night before, "We're holding our breath and crossing our fingers, and those who know how to pray are praying pretty hard." That night I asked my grandmother Mamie, sitting hunched up on the edge of her bed, what she thought about the children going to school together. "Oh, son, I don't know," she said. "I just don't know. But I think they'll get along fine, if people'll just let 'em alone."

7

January 7, 1970, dawned clear and bitterly cold, a cold that rarely comes to Mississippi. It was 16 degrees on South Main Street, the trees along the older avenues were seared and deathly, and the water in the potholes of the roads in the Negro sections was frozen solid. All over Yazoo there was a cold eerie calm.

The "nationals" were out in force, for Yazoo is only forty-eight miles from the Jackson airport, and with its fifty-fifty population and its origins in both the hills and the delta, this was where the stories would go out from that day, telling the nation and many parts of the world how the first major test of massive school integration in America in a district with a black majority would work in a "typical Mississippi town." The *New York Times* was there, and the Washington *Post,* the TV networks, the wire services, the Boston *Globe, Time,* the Detroit *News,* and the Chicago *Sun-Times.*

At my high school, whites and blacks waited on the grounds or walked inside in separate groups; two police cars were parked nearby. I drove into the Negro section of town to the old black high school, which today was to become the town's junior high; across the street was a previously black grade school, about to become grades four and five for whites and blacks. (Three years or so ago, I gave a talk to the black high school, to a sea of black faces, and gave five autographed copies of *Invisible Man* to the school library. A white lady who was there came up to me later and said, "Who were you talkin' to? The little niggers didn't understand you," and I said I guessed I was talking to one person, and that was myself.) Cars were parked in all directions, some with Confederate flags on their windows or bumpers, and parents of both races were bringing their children into the school buildings. Roy Reed of the *Times,* a *Times* photographer, and I stood outside the front entrance to the junior high; we were soon to be joined by the Boston *Globe.* I went inside, to try to get a seat at the first meeting of the new student body of the amalgamated Yazoo Junior High.

"Winkie!" a booming voice shouted in my direction, using the nickname I have not been called since the sixth grade. "You're not allowed in there." I was escorted out by a man I did not recognize, rejoining the nationals at the front door. In a few moments, a Yazoo cop with the dimensions of any of the L.A.

Rams' front four, who would make Rod Steiger in *In the Heat of the Night* seem benign and nunlike in comparison, came up to our group and shouted, *"You from the press?"* Without waiting for anyone's answer, he said, "The minute somebody tells you move, you *move!"*

"No one's asked us to move yet, Officer," Reed of the *Times,* who traverses the South forever, as a man seeking lost and holy visions, a wandering nomad of the Arab tribe of Sulzberger, said, with some dignity.

"Move if anybody says move," the cop repeated, then drifted away. I remembered him from the Greyhound station fourteen years before, when I was putting a friend on the midnight bus stopping briefly here between Memphis and New Orleans. He got on the bus with a flashlight and went up and down the aisle, and when he came out, I asked him if there was any trouble. "No," he had said, "I was lookin' to see if any niggers were sittin' up front."

By now the school assembly had begun, and everything was oppressively quiet. It was much the same all over town. At one of the grade schools later, black and white children were playing together in the schoolyard. One group, dancing in a circle for ring-around-a-rosy, were all white, but in the circle next to them white and Negro children held hands and kicked their feet. Over in the high school, where a meeting of the student body was taking place, the situation was slightly more dramatic. In a new twist, all the black students sat together in the front seats of the auditorium, and all the whites sat together in the back. When the student-body president of the black high school was introduced, the Negroes applauded loudly and gave the black-power gesture, the raised fist. When the white president was introduced, he received a sturdy round of support from the back seats. The white principal spoke sternly about discipline. When the black principal (now the *assistant* principal) stood to quote from the Scriptures about the necessity of education, there were the sudden makings of an incident; he has a physical deformity, and a number of the white students laughed out loud.

By the middle of the day, however, it was quite apparent that Yazoo City had indeed integrated its schools calmly and deliberately, and that some 80 per cent of all the white children had chosen to stay.* Only two white teachers in the town had resigned. With the attrition to the private school, there was a black majority in every school, beginning with about 60 per cent in the high school and increasing toward the lower grades.

The nationals filed their stories, and within the next two days the town was praised on front pages, by the news weeklies, and by all the television networks. A Justice Department lawyer in Jackson said that Yazoo City had shown more strength in its schools

*The total enrollment in the city dropped by 480; 2,077 blacks and 1,362 whites began the new semester together.

than any other district in Mississippi, and pointed in contrast to the town of Canton just thirty miles away, where the white leaders and merchants had literally succeeded in destroying their public schools. The *Herald's* editorials were captioned, "We Should Be Proud," and "Yazooans Show Character," and an outpouring of letters was published from all over the country. A typical one, from R. D. Cheatham, former star wingback on the Yazoo Indians of my era, now living in Las Vegas, said, "I have never been so proud of my home town than when I saw [the editor and the school superintendent] express a dynamic understanding of the changes taking place and Yazoo City's positive reaction to them. The coming months will not be easy, but I want you to know that I applaud your initial efforts. . . ." Another outside correspondent wrote, "We have been listening to the Yazoo City story on TV. We wish to commend you for your efforts. May Yazoo City lead the South out of its dreadful impasse." A white lady said to my mother, "When I read all the good things about integration here, it scares me. When I read anything critical, it makes me mad."

In the following days, an uneasy calm would settle on the town, an emotional labor survived but scarcely overcome. "ALL'S WELL IN YAZOO CITY, BUT WHAT ABOUT TOMORROW?" the Memphis *Commercial Appeal* wrote as its headline to a highly pessimistic analysis reporting that some white leaders "would rather judgment could be withheld. They do not appreciate the conclusions, however laudatory, reached in the fleeting moments of deadline by the correspondents from Detroit, Washington, St. Louis, New York, and even Copenhagen." The Memphis paper's pessimism was not entirely ill-founded. On the day after school integration, officials from the Justice Department in Jackson were in Yazoo to find out why its school officials had retained essentially the same classroom structure as before, which largely meant segregated classrooms in integrated buildings. There would be seeds of future trouble here, leading later to another NAACP suit.

But the predictions of the white conservatives had not materialized. Yazoo City came into a new era with remarkably strong and resilient leadership from both races, and while a number of other Mississippi schools, the first thirty districts in the national test, were being abandoned altogether to the blacks, the people of Yazoo would look ahead with considerable realism. "We've got to hold the whites," a young lawyer said. "This semester is critical. If we can hold them now, we can hold them from now on. And by God, I think we're going to do it." They saw few grand historical designs in what they had accomplished; they were more than willing to live with their experiment one day at a time. There had been, after all, a straightforward simplicity, a stark logic, in this act of compliance. Had the warnings of the white racists over the generations been so true?

The white high school had purchased an expensive machine, some time before, to spray the dressing rooms in the gymnasium and other places against athlete's-foot germs and the like. "I saw them put that big spray machine in the back of a pickup truck to take over to the colored school so they could spray it down before the white children started to school there," a white man told me. "When I saw them take that spray machine to the colored school, that was the day I knew integration was finally comin' after all the talk that it wouldn't—finally comin' after all."*

---

*Also, the black grade school had used a cowbell rather than an electrical bell system. This too was remedied before the advent of the whites.

8

At the start of the school year in September of 1969, the Manchester Academy, the all-white private school which held its classes in churches and paid them a nominal rent, had an enrollment of 335 students through the first nine grades. After the public schools were integrated, Manchester added the three highest grades and increased its enrollment over a month's period to about 800. Tuition was expensive for this area: $500 a year for the first child, $400 for the second, and with a campaign on to build a new school, the costs would be even more burdensome.* A wealthy lumberman donated the land for the building, which would be ready by September of 1970, but to raise the necessary $600,000 Manchester would assess pledges of one-tenth of the 1969 gross family income of each family that had

*Since 1964, parents in Mississippi could get a state grant of $240 per child for private schooling, but that of course has been ruled unconstitutional.

children enrolled in the school, with eight years to pay. There was no promise that proper academic accreditation would follow. Many whites were further concerned that the building program, the tuition, and the public school taxes would place too severe a strain on the town's economic structure, and they argued that Yazoo, which is by no means a wealthy place, could only bear so much. But it was at least clear that the presence of the private schools, in Yazoo and all over Mississippi, served as a safety valve against violent resistance when serious integration finally came.

A few days after the public schools integrated, the private school held one of a series of receptions for their new students and parents at the Calvary Baptist Church on Jackson Avenue. About forty people were there, and they milled around in the hutch-like rooms of the church annex. They were moderately well dressed, and clean and scrubbed, and all of them, in this week that the public schools were courting amalgamation and the degeneration of the race, were smiling and cheerful. It was a going-to-church smile, the mood you get in a Manhattan polling place on Election Day—an air of duty being performed, of eye-to-eye accord, of a rather pleasant unctuousness. A female chemistry and physics teacher, who had been a substitute teacher in the public schools, explained how she must somehow arrive at a compromise curriculum for students coming to Manchester Academy from three or four different public schools with as many different textbooks. She might not be able to provide a physics course, she complained, because she wouldn't have enough students. But there was an optimistic tone to her talk, and she pointed out that the Presbyterians had built themselves a new annex recently as a facility to accommodate private school students if that proved necessary, as indeed it had.

A mother, exceedingly tall and thin, with a line of lipstick so clear that one had never seen such a well-delineated mouth, talked about her two boys. One of them was very bookish. "He just keeps readin'; he puts his nose in a book and he doesn't look right or left." Because of this unusual concentration, she said, he wouldn't see a Negro anyway, so with one more semester to go before he graduates, she left him in Yazoo High School. "The other boy, though, just can't take it, he just can't stand niggers, so I'm sendin' him to private school. It's gonna be so rough. I can't pay for it. My mama and aunt are payin' for it. I guess it's somethin' we'll just have to accept." Another mother joined the group and complained similarly about the costs of enrolling her two sons. "Johnny had the sense to take his textbooks with him from the public school," she said, "but that fool Billy didn't."

As the conversation in the room grew more lively and agreeable, there was much talk about "nigger odors . . . the way they smell and all." A thin, weathered old woman, with a body too fragile to support her basso voice, was one of the first white teachers to resign from a public school out in the county. She said, "It almost killed me when the nigger teachers came. They took over the teachers' lounge and the washrooms and used the commodes and everything. I never saw such carryin' on."

The big old boys who were there stood off by themselves in a corner, chewing gum and looking trapped and unhappy. If you have seen big growing boys in a social group of females surrounded by vociferous mothers in a place they do not want to be, you can imagine the crass liberties they felt were being taken with their burgeoning but untested masculinity. Would the Manchester Academy have a football team someday? If so, would the Yazoo High Indians, black and white Indians now, deign to play against these big, glum-looking boys? And with what embarrassing consequences?

I had always expected that the churches, in some form, might move into education down here before it was over, and there was a faintly religious aspect to Yazoo's private school in its organizational phase. From our rudimentary reading of the history of the race, we all know of the old tradition of summoning the church against the civil authority, of the church as a source of countervailing power and protection against all the alien, evil exercises in the secular. In Mississippi, where, with notable individual exceptions, the church had remained institutionally a bulwark against racial integration, against the distinctly secular threat of what the descendants of the Yazoo slaves of six generations ago might do to one's middle-class Christianity, one sensed this was happening after all. Going to school in the basements and annexes of the Protestant churches, the private school children of Yazoo had isolated themselves in churchly sanctuaries, far removed from the difficult historic events through which their town was living. *"I was glad when they said unto me, Let us go into the house of the Lord."* But if the Lord had chosen to come farther than Memphis, as the tenant farmer Ben McGee requested, it is worth asking, would he have gone public or private?

9

The DeCells

Herman DeCell is the state senator from Yazoo, Sharkey, and Issaquena Counties. In 1967, he was elected by about 350 votes out of 12,000, and he concedes that his active stand on behalf of the public schools and his generally moderate position on race may hurt him when he comes up again in '71. He is a graduate of the Harvard Law School, a pleasant and thoughtful man in his forties, full of life's vicissitudes as an intellectual in the tough arena, but also aware of the need for good enjoyment and civil talk. He has deliberated a great deal about politics and social change and, like his wife, is passionately devoted to making Yazoo a better place. His wife, Harriet, is a handsome blonde who teaches in the high school, where their daughter Alice is editor of the school paper and a leader among the liberal white students. It is rumored around town that Alice has read *Soul on Ice.*

There is a dinner party at their house the night before the integration deadline. I am straight down from New York, and the Mississippi accents all around are exceptionally warm and reassuring to one who has spent a winter in the chill East. Mississippi accents of both races are probably the most soft and tender of all the American ways of speaking, and if one does not watch it they will mesmerize you and lull the brain, so that you will listen very closely without paying attention. The DeCells are the only people in town who subscribe to the *New York Times.* "I thought the library subscribes," someone remarks, and Harriet replies, "Well, we give the library our copy."

A couple of the nationals are there, and it is a pleasant evening, with good food and sophisticated conversation. The lines of civilization are very thin indeed, but here in this house, at the edge of the delta, these people who are involved deeply in politics and in the realities of their town have made for themselves a place of civility and grace. We speak at some length about this town which we know best, about people out of the past whom we all remember, about the intrigues and passions and foibles of fifteen years ago.

The senator, who is apprehensive that an established dual school system, public and private, black and white, might become the reality here, believes there are several good reasons why Yazoo has been acting more reasonably than other delta towns. Owen

Cooper's chemical plant with its six hundred employees, the enlightened local industry, is one reason. There has not been as much civil rights friction here in the past as in other places. An active white group drove out the Klan some years ago. And the weekly newspaper has been consistently responsible. "If it weren't for Bubba Mott [the editor]," Herman says, "we might have the National Guard at every desk tomorrow."

The high school up to now has had about 15 per cent Negro enrollment under freedom-of-choice. Harriet describes one white teacher of somewhat conservative views "who goes on for hours about how nice her bright Negro children are and how raunchy her bad white children are." From her experience, teaching in the Negro school and the tokenly integrated white school, she believes that if all the white and black students had to be divided into three groups by testing and grades, the top group would be almost entirely white with a few exceptions, the bottom would be black with a few exceptions, but in the vast middle group there would be a strong overlap amounting to about half and half. I ask her what she has felt most strongly about what has been happening here:

"I have a consciousness that small things fit together into big puzzles, and that one is responsible for one's actions and had better be ready to accept it. You get tired of getting up every day and wondering if you're being challenged by your environment. You can live in a small town and be sorry for yourself that the world passes you by—and suddenly you realize that the world isn't passing you by at all—that it's all here. We've got a lot of friends in big cities, and they seem to be beating their heads against the wall all the time. That's not so true here. One individual can affect a small town. At least you can decide what you believe and stand for it. I can remember a lot of failure. It's not too bad to try and fail. When I don't try, it bothers me deeply."

NORMAN MOTT

Bubba Mott, the editor of the *Herald,* is, like Herman DeCell, from one of the older families, as they say here. It has not, I know, been easy for him. If they give a Pulitzer Prize for an editor who speaks from deep inside himself, from travail and a personal recommitment, then he deserves it. I remember him from my own boyhood; he is a rare man, rare especially for Mississippi, who has grown into middle age, suddenly and without one's expecting it, into a complicated human being, and a tough editor in the finest tradition of small-town American journalism. His great-great-grandmother was the first white child born in Yazoo County, and the paper has belonged to his family since 1914. The reaction to his editorials on school integration, he says, "has been more favorable than unfavorable." He is a graduate of Ole Miss, and had been a fairly strong conservative in the past. The big change in his feelings came during the Meredith episode at Ole Miss in 1962. He thought Ross Barnett and John Satterfield and the others were "really leading us" when they said the 1954 decision could be circumvented on legal grounds. "This was when I became aware that legal segregation had no basis. People would say, 'The Lord made 'em black, we didn't.' I went around the coffee shops talking with people about this. I didn't know until after the Meredith case. This is what gets me. I didn't know we were whistling up the wind. *I didn't know.* If Yazoo City can be the example I think it can be—and I'm not alone in this—to have a town in the best interests of *all* the citizens, if this can be made to work anywhere in America, it will be made here." Then he adds, with a self-mocking twist of the head: "But I'm not sure."

HAROLD KELLEY

"Hardwood" Kelley, as we used to call him when he was our basketball coach eighteen years ago, is superintendent of the city school system now. He was fresh out of Ole Miss as a basketball star then, just a kid and not too much older than we, though we didn't know it. He was an immense favorite among us, especially when he would say, just before we roared out onto the court in our red, white, and black jerseys for a game against Belzoni or Satartia or Indianola or Canton, "Boys, hang loose as a goose!" and for the flair with which he would make fools of us with his dribbles and hook shots in practice to remind us who was boss. Coaches are very important to adolescent boys, for they are examples and ideals, they siphon off the terrible adolescent fears, they provide a sport and organize an alternative to the dark private sexuality of the boy. It is not an ignoble calling.

One night many years ago in the Delta Valley Conference finals against Cleveland from Bolivar County, before a packed crowd of 1,000 in the Yazoo gymnasium, we found ourselves matched with a six-foot-nine center named Brown, who had averaged 30 points a game. "Hardwood" Kelley devised a floating defense that kept the unlikely giant Brown bottled up against the defensive skills of Big Boy Wilkinson, Muttonhead Shepherd, and Bubba Barrier, but left a bull-legged football player named Slick McCool, who seldom could hit the backboard, wide open most of the game. McCool made 25 points and we lost. Even as a grown man, late at night sometimes in Manhattan, I am obsessed by Slick McCool, wide open and hitting his tawdry jump shots.

Coach Kelley and I were sitting in his big sunny office on Calhoun Avenue several days after the schools had integrated. He had dark circles under his eyes, and though he has changed remarkably little from the boy he was eighteen years ago, he was plainly a totally exhausted man. In Mississippi and many other small towns in America, coaches, if they are smart, become principals, and then superintendents. I knew he was not a racist, but I wondered how he might have adapted. He showed me the figures on the 80 per cent showing of the whites who stayed in the schools. "This is a complete social revolution," he said. "We're losin' and pickin' up. Some of the kids who didn't come the first day are moving in. Some are moving out. I was surprised to have as many stay as did. That was the result of some hard work. I think we surprised the national press. They didn't think we'd comply."

He and the other school officials had gone to New Orleans to argue before the Fifth Circuit on the October Supreme Court decision. "I was sitting there when Judge Bell started his speech. The judge said, 'You're down here to hear me tell you what you've got to do. I ask you to listen, and ask questions, but there won't be any arguments.' It was that cold. I got completely weak wonderin' how I was going to do it. But we came home and organized our staff and got down to it."

On the question of segregated classrooms, the old coach would not be pressed. "This has been based on educational reasons, and we've told the Justice Department that. In September, at the first of a school year, this sort of thing wouldn't have been a problem. We've changed a whole school system in less than a month. I think we did a good job, Negro and white. Under our present setup, I think we can maintain a school system people will like—if the courts will leave us alone."

The buzzer rang, and Hardwood Kelley picked up the telephone. The conversation concerned how traffic should be directed around the schools, and he gave some orders and hung up. "That's typical," he said. "One wrong word and you've had it. That's how delicate it is. With the situation as fluid as it is, one false move would blow it sky high. I know I've done all I could to keep it together. Now it's time to go to school and get down to business. You know what I mean, Willie."

FATHER O'LEARY

Father Malcolm O'Leary calls himself a "black Irishman." He is rector of the Negro Catholic church, St. Francis, and up until quite recently he had been the effective leader of the town's blacks, but now he has been squeezed out of that position; some of the more militant blacks have begun to call him a "white man."

He is a big light-skinned Negro, full of self-laughter, and there is a soft gentleness to him, a conscious tenderness; you know after talking with him that he lacks some of the spite and toughness to be a leader here, that he knows this, and that he is a highly intelligent man who wants to do best by everybody. He is only thirty-nine, and he is not wearing the priest's collar to talk with me. He is a native of an adjoining county where his father was a carpenter, and a graduate of several priests' colleges and of Catholic University in Washington. He came to Yazoo briefly in 1963 doing some civil rights work, and he returned permanently in 1967. We were sitting in the recreation room of his rectory, a spacious room almost bare of furniture, with a picture of Jesus on the wall, Jesus in one of his most benign poses, and in the late afternoon we were in the half-dark, with the beginnings of a full delta moon out the window.

He talked about his first trip here seven years ago. "That's when I first met Russell [Ardis Russell, the police chief]. The cops literally followed me around for six weeks. They stopped me down in front of Hugh Pickett's house, you know, Hugh Pickett's house? I had a brand-new driver's license but hadn't signed it yet. Russell looked at the license and asked me something. I answered, 'Yes.' He said, 'Say yessir to me, nigger.' He said he'd beat my head in and chase me out of town. He knew everything about me, where I came from and everything. The sisters here at the church were worried I'd be hurt. But as long as they didn't hit me, I'd be all right. If they hit me, they'd probably have a little fight."

When he came back in '67, he saw the town was changing. Police Chief Russell had kicked a seventeen-year-old black girl, and Father O'Leary heard about it and filed a suit. "One day later I was in City Hall and Russell called out to me. He cursed me and said, 'What's this about you takin' that nigger girl to file a suit? You nothin' but a damned agitator.' I said, 'I'm not an agitator, I'm a Catholic priest.' 'Well, you're still a damned agitator,' he said. Some of the other cops were in the next room and when they heard all this they laughed real hard. I think this broke the ice."

Two years ago, Father O'Leary, acting independently but supported by the NAACP, started trying to get the white stores in town to hire blacks. Symbolically, the first business to do so was the Black & White Dry Goods Store on Main Street. But the others were adamant. He also pressed demands before the mayor for two Negro policemen, two firemen, and two clerks in the city government. The mayor said, "That's a threat. I'll do it in time." Later, when the town complied with these demands, the demands were increased to twenty-five. The Negro community organized their economic boycott after a series of mass meetings with O'Leary as the leader. One of the methods for enforcing the boycott, he said, had been public spankings of those blacks who defied it. "Then Charles Evers persuaded Rudy Shields and George Collins to take over from me because they thought I was being too lenient.

"Yazoo is not like some of these other towns," he said. "Beneath the surface I don't think relations are so bad. The bad part's all been *on* the surface.

"I tell the white man not to worry over the integration in the schools. The white girl won't be abused unless she throws herself at the blacks; then they'll stand in line. My real fear is that the involvement of white boys and black girls will get worse, because they'll start younger. I fear the abuse of black girls by white boys."

RUDY SHIELDS

The NAACP headquarters is not the most impressive house in town, but it may be, in terms of a general pulling power, the most influential. It is a shabby frame structure on West Powell Street in the Negro section, undistinguished from any of the other houses on the block, with sharply inclined stairs leading onto a small unpainted porch. Inside is a small front room littered with paper coffee cups. A semi-automatic carbine stands in the corner, and there is a picture of Martin Luther King over the gas heater in the fireplace. A sign on the wall says, "Don't talk politics in here unless you are a registered voter." A big-screen television set is tuned to CBS News, which is covering at this moment the integration of the schools in Hattiesburg, 150 miles south of here. A large group of whites are chanting, *"Hell no, we won't go."*

George Collins, a farmer who grew up near here, is the president of the local NAACP; he is a warily apprehensive man in tinted glasses. "We been over the barrel for two hundred years," he says to me. "Now we've got the man where we need him and we can't take no promises. Black people are not gonna be pushed around any more." He says this with a strong Mississippi Negro accent, looking over at me with sharp, fleeting glances, obviously not too happy I am here. He does not know who I am, and I don't think he would care if he did.

It is apparent from the start, however, that the effective leader of the Yazoo blacks, because of the way people defer to him casually, is the very black, self-assured, well-built, and outwardly mean-tempered (but not as mean as he may think he is) young man who has been sitting next to Collins and who darts into a side room every time the telephone rings. His name is Rudy Shields. He has been carrying on a series of interrupted conversations with the NAACP Legal Defense Fund lawyers in Jackson. This is the afternoon the schools integrated, and the word is out that the classrooms had remained segregated throughout the school system. "The way they sold it to the whites was that they wouldn't be in the same classes," Shields says. "If a court order comes through now, I expect a mass white walkout."

Rudy Shields is thirty-nine years old, a native of Columbus, Ohio, an experienced civil rights activist in Chicago, a protégé of Charles Evers ("All I've learned I've learned from Evers"), and a veteran of five years of organizational work in Mississippi. He has organized, he says, thirty economic boycotts all over the state, and has also been active in voter registration. About 40 per cent of the blacks in the county, he says, have been registered. He was called in from Belzoni to take over the direction of the boycott here from Father O'Leary. Among the whites here, he is the anathema. On the race issue, it is peculiarly Southern to have a devil, a personification of all the disruption; remove him from the scene, and everything will be all right. "I saw Shields walk into a restaurant," a white man had said to me, "and I'll tell *you,* he's not the kind of person I'd want in *my* home." His name comes up in most conversations with white leaders; he is very much on their mind. An NAACP lawyer told me, "Rudy Shields is one of the few black radicals left who still believe in integration."

He would be handsome, in almost a straightforward way, but something is missing. There is a physical expression to his face—something developed, I think—which destroys conventional good looks. He slurs over his words, he deliberately speaks in the Mississippi Negro talk, his lips are slightly misshapen. I was introduced to him after having been told he was *the militant* here, and he had said, "We know who you are." He is the professional black leader, but he plainly wanted to talk with me, the white boy from Yazoo; he is full of a kind of watchful curiosity, and I am sure he speaks more toughly than he feels.

"We urge our people in really strong language to

enforce the boycott," he says. "People phone here to get permission even if they have to go to a doctor. They make sure they don't make a mistake. I've seen greater black unity here than anyplace in the country with the exception of Port Gibson. In Mississippi I've learned this, working with Charles Evers. First, you have to get the fear out of them—their fear of the policemen more than anything else. Second, people tend to rally around a man, not an organization. They'll follow him if they think he's got guts.

"Yazoo has great potential. It's the first community in the state to stand up for public schools to this extent. A lot of whites have put their prestige on the line here. I think these young whites here—say, under the age of twenty-five—are going to try to make this work. It's been good to see the changes in the community, though I've seen the white power structure say they'd *never* have a black policeman, or a black fireman. This was before the boycott. I've seen whites show more respect to blacks in individual ways than before the boycott.

"This state will solve its racial problems quicker than any state. Economic boycotts and voter registration are more effective here. In the North with the big corporations, you don't know *who* to attack. I do think the Black Panthers in Chicago are the most effective way to deal with the situation there. But the Southern white man is more *honest* than in the North. At least you know where he stands. I used to be anti-white. I didn't trust the Northern white workers who came down here. They were like carpetbaggers. But the young kids now, all over the country, are proving their commitment. Racism in the North is more complex and subtle than it is here."

The gas heater hissed away in the fireplace and Shields left to take another call. There was a sound of footsteps on the porch, and a voice shouted, "We the *cops,* and this here's a *raid!*" Then the door opened and several Negroes came in, going to various parts of the house, or stretching out in the overstuffed chairs. An older man came in and asked for Shields. When Shields returned, the man explained he had a suit in the Modernized Cleaners, but that he had been to St. Louis and didn't know the Modernized Cleaners was being boycotted.

"All right, go ahead and get your suit," Shields said, "but don't take it there again."

"No, I won't," the visitor replied, then offered to renew his NAACP membership card. Shields told him where to pay.

"So it's all right to get that suit, ain't it?" the man persisted.

"Yessir."

A few weeks before, when the town hired two black policemen after pressure from the boycott, Shields was at the City Hall and confronted one of the hireling cops. A reporter overheard the exchange.

"Well," Shields said, eying him up and down, "I see you got your own uniform."

"It fits," the black cop said. "It's fine."

"That badge, it looks small. How come they don't give you a big badge?"

"A good man don't need a big badge," the rookie said.

" . . . and this little ole pistol. That big enough to do the job?"

"Try me," the cop said.

JOHN OAKES

A thin old man with a wrinkled face and a long and mournful look came into the room from the back of the house. John Oakes was born and raised here, graduated from Fisk, and studied economics at the University of Chicago in the 1940s. Once he dropped by my office in New York to talk about Yazoo, and he submitted an article refuting Professor Galbraith on the Keynesian economics. He is setting up a shoe factory in town, capitalized by blacks and whites, with a $135,000 loan secured by white banks. It is his life's dream, and it will employ almost 150 Negroes.

Oakes joined the conversation. "Sure school integration will work here," he said. "Of course, it's irrelevant. You put an investment on all those heads and they all end up in Chicago anyway."

He started talking to Shields about the one million

blacks on relief in New York. "Blacks have to create their own wealth," he said, standing to full height, gesturing with both hands. "That's the key to it, Mr. Shields. That's it. That tells the whole story." Then he swiftly changed the subject. He said, with reference to nothing, that the Yazoo *Herald* had started running "Mr." and "Mrs." in front of Negro names; it even ran a picture of a black man in a Jackson hospital who later died. "Yeah, that's one less Tom," Shields said. Oakes ignored him, at least momentarily, for this seemed heady talk. Then they discussed systems vs. individuals in various societies and the use of force to achieve certain ends. "Of course," Shields said, "we don't use force in making sure everybody keeps the boycott."

"He's got his tongue in his cheek," Oakes said, roaring with a most astounding belly laugh. "It's so far in his cheek he's about to swallow it."

I had left my own car two blocks up the gravel road from the NAACP office, in front of Father O'Leary's rectory. The moon was now high over the delta, the lights flickered gently for as far as I could see, and as I walked along the road I noticed a car, parked fifty yards away at a small intersection. The car slowly pulled away from the side road and turned in to the one I was walking on. As it approached me, its lights still out, I could see that four men were in it, two in the front seat, two in the back, and when they got within twenty-five yards of me, they turned on their lights and slowed down even more. One of the men opened the back door and slammed it again.

This is it, I said to myself; my premonition had been right all along. In a few seconds, they would open the door and stick out a .12-gauge shotgun. I was seized with a dreadful, bone-chilling fear. I felt dizzy, my head curiously light and giddy, and I fought the urge to bolt and run; I would die face forward on my home ground with some shred of Southern dignity.

The car was now even with me. Then it continued down the road after its own business.

I was feeling, at this point, relieved and damned silly when, about fifty yards from my car, a pack of ten or twelve hound dogs emerged from around the chinaberry tree at the side of a Negro house and headed in my direction. They were clearly under the spell of the January delta moon, walking on their toes, spinning around on themselves, sniffing mutual asses, snapping at each other behind the ears, howling and barking all the while at nothing in particular —a great whirling mob of animal flesh going in circles and tangents. I remembered from my boyhood how Negro dogs acted in a group, like national reporters traveling in a pack after the same story; they are full of fire and willing to act against any white man on a moment's notice. One of the dogs spotted me, and did not hesitate to signal the others. They paused for a moment, giving me a chance to race for the car; then they were hot on my trail, unleashing an ungodly Negro-dog wail, the sound of shrill and distant echoes merging. As I reached the car, opened the door, and jumped inside, several of the hound dogs jumped up on the doors. One tried to climb on the hood but fell off in a heap. I pulled the car away and left the old Yazoo dogs to their nocturnal moon-spangled peregrinations, presumably the only violent resisters my Yankee premonition would have to deal with, at least on this trip.

WALTER BRIDGFORTH

He is the courtly conservative lawyer, a gentleman Tory given to quoting literature on almost any subject, and as the attorney for the public schools in the county system, he has had his brushes with the young lawyers from the United States Department of Justice. Bridgforth is widely read in the Southern manner of, say, a generation or so ago, a man who, were he a delta planter, could write a book much like William Alexander Percy's *Lanterns on the Levee,* which was a great Southern testament in the 1940s. He used to give speeches at our assemblies in high school, inspiring us to read books, which was good advice for intrepid young philistines, and one suspects, after talking with him here, that he is considerably more conservative than his words suggest, for he uses words with a sweetness and a civility that may take the rub off his innermost thoughts. We were having lunch at his house on a beautiful wooded hill out on the Benton Road. There is a smoky stillness in the air here, and far away down the hill the echo of an axe on wood.

He showed me a paragraph from a legal brief he had once filed:

School-board members are unpaid public servants. For almost fifteen years, members of Southern school boards have borne the abuse, both of idealists who assail them from secure ivory towers wreathed in moral righteousness on the one hand, and disadvantaged, bewildered, but often patriotic citizens on the other hand, who are driven against their will and against what they often consider their "rights." Historically, the conflict is like those which have raged through the years between rival religious sects. There is a ghostly parallel between some events of the day and those related by Sir Walter Scott in Wandering Willie's Tale, from *Redgauntlet.* Sir Walter has Willie say: "He was knighted at London court, wi' the King's ain sword; and being a red-hot prelatist, he came down here, rempauging like a lion, with commissions of lieutenancy (and of lunacy, for what I ken), to put down a' the Whigs and Covenanters in the county. Wild wark they made of it; for the Whigs were as dour as the Cavaliers were fierce, and it was which should first tire the other."

"These people in the Republican Administration," he says over lunch, "have really tried to give us a break, more than our cousin Lyndon did, but they've been subjected to pressures and they're running scared." A twenty-nine-year-old Justice Department lawyer in Jackson had said to him the other day, "We're completing the Reconstruction of the South."

But the Justice lawyers under Nixon are better to deal with than the L.B.J. ones, he says. "At least they cut their hair." Bridgforth spoke of the need for more and better vocational training in the schools, of grouping by ability. He spoke bitterly, with a soft, resigned contempt, of the federal government, of Secretary Finch's recent attacks on the Southern private schools. Yet he had come through it all to acknowledge the inevitability of the growing federal power.

In a sudden expression of change which was characteristic of many of the white conservatives I would see, and which I doubt would have happened under the circumstances a few years back, Bridgforth then said, "Five years from now we'll have a better, more effective school system than we have today. The parallel is that there will be more and better private schools. These probably won't be Citizens Councils schools, either. If they're wise, they'll do what the private schools of the East do, represent all ethnic and class groups. And if we don't fall out in the meantime, I believe in ten years we'll have a better community."

John Satterfield

In the main reception room of the large new building perched on the last reluctant hill before the delta begins, there were eleven paintings of extremely happy darkies. The Freedom Summer of 1964 has largely passed them by. They are strumming banjos,

71

picking cotton, eating watermelon, and sitting on front porches near the big house watching the boll weevils grow.

John Satterfield, who was president of the American Bar Association in 1961–62, has an office on one of the top floors. A CBS camera crew had just left. Satterfield has been the foremost legal advocate of segregated schools in the state, a close friend of Senators Eastland and Stennis, and it is this staunch conservatism which made him a controversial president of the ABA.

I had seen him before on a national television interview, where he came across as rather suspicious, elusive, and even rude, and I was surprised to find him the paragon of Old South gentility. We talked about the Civil War here, about our relatives who came from the little town of Port Gibson, about Myres McDougal of the Yale Law School against whom Satterfield had competed years ago for a Rhodes scholarship. "Myres won the Rhodes and got to Yale, and I got to be president of the ABA." He offered me a cigar, and later invited me to lunch at Danrie's Restaurant. The conservative white South has hung on through its lawyers and politicians, and no one knows this better than Satterfield. He is thin and craggy, and if it were not for the unexpected mischief in his eye, he would look very much like the cartel men in Chaplin's *Modern Times.* When he discusses the issue at hand, it is not with the grace of our amiable social exchange, but with a stringent legalism, a cautious parsimony.

He was "surprised and shocked" by the October Supreme Court decision. "This was the first time in the history of education in the United States that the Court has declined to follow the recommendations of the federal education authorities, the state and local authorities, the Justice Department, and the attorney general of the state, and rendered a decree opposite to their recommendations.

"I'm hopeful but doubtful of the success of integration under these recent decisions. In Yazoo City all of us have done all we can to keep the situation smooth and carry out the determinants of the Court. I don't think we'll have any violence. But we have the experience of other areas. One illustration: when Congress adopted the federal statute subsequent to the *Brown* decision applicable to the schools in the District of Columbia, President Eisenhower welcomed the opportunity of integrating the public schools, and in the best atmosphere possible in the country. As we all know, the public schools in Washington are now about ninety-three per cent black. I've spoken in forty-eight of the fifty states and met with lawyers in every state and observed the attitudes of the people. The attitudes in Yazoo City don't differ materially from the attitudes of people all over the United States, including the District of Columbia."

If the schools work in Yazoo, he concedes, the situation could be excellent for the entire community. "The Negro leadership among the citizens of Yazoo County is very good. I limit that to actual citizens of Yazoo County as distinguished from persons sent in by organizations from other areas. I won't mention names, but one of the most active leaders who's been used to intimidate Negro citizens here was also used in Port Gibson for the same purpose." This intimidation has taken the form of threatening phone calls, damaging businesses owned by Negroes, "public cursing of Negro and white women," and "stationing toughs on street corners."

And what if the actual classroom structure in the various schools were desegregated under a further Court order? He paused for a moment, puffed on his cigar, and gazed out the window at the flat brown terrain, at the dead cotton stalks stretching toward the horizon. He replied, sternly, "We won't have any violence here, but if such an action were taken, it would hasten the day when this school district might experience the same results as Washington, D.C."

JEPPIE BARBOUR

When the mayor of Yazoo City was a very small child, he would go to Lintonia Park with the bigger boys to watch us play our particularly jarring brand of tackle football. One afternoon, a group of Negro boys our age, walking in a pack across the white section, stopped by the park. We milled around in a hopping, jumping mass, talking football, showing off for each other, and sounding for all the world, with our deliberately accentuated expressions, like much the same race. We organized an interracial scrimmage, and the cops came by in their patrol car and ordered us to break it up.

Now the cops work for Jeppie. He was elected mayor at the age of twenty-seven, defeating Harry Applebaum, who had been mayor fourteen years. When I was in high school, Harry Applebaum directed traffic at Jefferson and Main every Saturday night, an exercise, much like Lincoln's walking over to the War Department building at night during the Civil War, which must have eased in some small measure the pressures of power. At a party in Yazoo three years before, the editor of *Commentary,* Norman Podhoretz, who had come along with me to see the South, was conversing in a corner with a white citizen and suddenly shouted across the room at me, "Goddamnit, you didn't tell me Yazoo City has a Jewish mayor!"

Jeppie Barbour comes from a family of prominent Mississippi lawyers and jurists, but he dropped out of law school at Ole Miss and was working in the Delta National Bank when he ran for mayor. He is a fleshy young man with a smooth, open, innocent face. We were having some fish for lunch in the back room at Danrie's, and Jeppie complained about the Negro boycott. "South Main Street's dryin' up," he said, and listed the stores that had gone out of business, including one drugstore hit hardest "because it specialized in chitlin' sandwiches and two-dollar pistols." The Negro leaders in charge now "are completely irresponsible. They're determined to destroy the whites economically. That's totally unreasonable. Unfortunately they've got the support of the colored community now. This Rudy Shields is a professional agitator brought in to keep the pressure on. George Collins and Shields and these people will keep this boycott as long as they can. They're *enjoyin'* it. They've got enough of these punks runnin' around, smashin' windows, that they're scared to death. If you were black, you could walk up Main Street and buy anything you wanted. But if you were black and eighty years old, these punks would prevent it." He described the three new industries that were shortly coming into town. "These are things the local whites have worked to get here. And still they're tryin' to wipe us out—not wipe us out, but get us on our knees so they can tell us what to do. I'll tell you, when I came into office I intended to get some paving and some sewage improvements for the colored, but now I can't get too enthusiastic about it. We're gonna have to take the attitude that we can't give any help to anybody who supports this group that's tryin' to destroy the city." The time might have come, he said, for the whites to retaliate with firings and other measures. He had written a statement which he was trying to decide to release, which said, "I believe that it is time for white people to take whatever economic countermeasures they personally consider appropriate. Specifically I suggest that they consider (1) supporting local merchants, especially those hurt worst by the boycott, (2) reconsidering their hiring practices, and (3) withholding contributions to charities or churches which are not supporting economic growth and harmony for Yazoo City."

A biracial commission had been in existence in Yazoo for some time, and the mayor discussed some of his problems there also. "Maybe five years ago," he said, "you could've appointed a colored man yourself. Now you simply can't get away with it. They're goin' to have to pick their own leaders. You could've gotten on radio five years ago using these very words, 'George Collins is this nigger we've appointed,' and could've gotten away with it. I guess they're just goin' through a state of being rebellious and hard-nosed and not listenin' to white people like they used to."

The town has seventeen policemen in all, which struck me as a substantial force for a town of 14,000, and Mace is standard equipment; the policemen carry it on their belts. "You get a drunk," Jeppie says; "you either get him to come with you or you have to manhandle him. You give him Mace and he'll want to go anywhere with you. It keeps that nigger's head in good shape."

Discipline has likewise been a problem with "the little niggers around town. One seven-year-old stole a pistol, but the chief has his own homemade juvenile-delinquency kit. He has a belt that's bigger than a Sam Browne belt, and he calls the parents and gets them to come down and take the kid into the basement and use the belt.

"We've got the best fire department in the state. If I tried to fire those two new Negro firemen, the fire chief would whip me." But it was a different matter with the two policemen. The mayor was suspicious that they had been sleeping on the job at night, so he cruised around for several hours with a squad of white cops. "Sure enough, I caught 'em myself asleep at three in the morning, behind the colored swimmin' pool. They're drivin' taxis now or somethin'."

He has two children, second- and third-graders, in private school. "We know this school integration is inevitable," he says, "and the level-heads have prevailed. We haven't had any violence, but two days ago I wouldn't have predicted it. There were too many tensions here. I think the social life of the schools will be private now. But I don't know. These kids will surprise you sometimes." The senior prom was canceled last year, after the boycott had started in May. "I was worried about the Negroes walking by the Legion hut where the dance was supposed to be, so they had it in Shay Hines' side yard in Carter." Football, however, may be another consideration entirely. It is a folk ritual down here, rooted in the deepest impulses of the people, of the blacks as well as the whites, and

Jeppie thinks the town will support its integrated high school team next fall largely because of a 190-pound halfback named Kramer. "He's the best runnin' back in the country. I think people will go, if just to see Kramer."

Jeppie and I talked a little longer about some people we knew, and I said, "Mr. Mayor, what's really going to happen here?" A look of grave and ponderous innocence crossed his broad face, and he said, summoning up something I doubt he had summoned before:

"We're gonna make the most of this. They're all here and we're all here. We're stuck. But we'll make the most of it because we've got to. It won't be any fun. We don't have many newcomers, and it's hard to leave here no matter what happens. We're not gonna have any mass exodus, black or white. They're here to stay and we're here to stay, and we don't have much other choice."

David "Deacon" Patenotte

Deacon Patenotte owns Patenotte's Grocery on North Grand Avenue, a small supermarket in the white section. There had been considerable talk about him among both whites and blacks, and with good reason. He is a member of the NAACP in Yazoo, and he is one of the few whites whose store has not been boycotted.

I met him at his house around the corner from the store, and we drank coffee and talked through most of a drab rainy afternoon. Children played in the yard next door, and when the fire truck came by on the street outside, its sirens on full blast, several cars and children on bicycles were following behind it to its destination, a ritual I had completely forgotten. We do not follow fire trucks in Manhattan.

He was born and raised and lived his forty-two years, he says, within two blocks of his store, graduated from the Catholic school, and for forty-two years has been a member of St. Mary's Catholic Church. "The Meredith thing up at Oxford did somethin' to me. We had a priest here then, Father Hunter, and he said, 'Deacon, what do you think about what happened at Ole Miss?' I said, 'Father, I think it's a disgrace.' Father Hunter had several little meetings with a few Catholic laymen here, about what the Catholic Church should do about the race issue. At first there were eight of us, but this dropped off to two or three. People were just scared to death then. They wouldn't even discuss the subject."

Deacon is a tall, red-faced man with pale eyes and a pot belly, who moves with a quick, catlike energy all around the little room; there is a pressure working somewhere in the gut. Later, when I returned to New York, he would write a long, thoughtful letter elaborating on our conversation, telling me how Catholicism had influenced his thinking, how he did not want to seem self-righteous, but look: here is a map the Yazoo Chamber of Commerce has published of all the public landmarks in town, and there is not a single Negro place included; and did I know the white segregated hospital does not even take Medicaid? And that when the bank published a photograph of all its employees in a Christmas ad in the *Herald,* they did not include the Negro janitor, Nathaniel April? He has agonized through all this in some deep private part of himself, and he wants to talk about it.

"I think it was Dr. King's death that caused me to become a life member," he says. "The day my check went through the bank, a lady asked my wife if I'd joined the NAACP. That's how quick the news got out of the bank. I guess I'm the only white member in Mississippi—no, that ain't true. Sister Joanne down at St. Clara's belongs, and my wife, and Father Hunter down in Natchez. Sometimes I go to the black church, and the bishop of the diocese was there one Sunday afternoon givin' the mass. He came out of the pulpit and he told the blacks there, 'There's an organization in Yazoo City that will seek your civil rights by all legal means. Father Kist here, your friend, has helped organize the NAACP. You as Catholic adults have a moral right to seek your civil rights. You as Catholic parents have a moral right to seek these civil rights for your children.'

"Well, when this boycott came, people assumed I generated it, because I wasn't boycotted. People said I just did it for myself, and things sort of warmed up here. Father O'Leary walked the streets of this town for a year and a half tryin' to get people to hire blacks. He never lost faith that some way could be found to work together. But the whites kept puttin' him off and puttin' him off. They kept sayin' they were thinkin' about a black policeman and various other things, but the mayor, Jeppie, said he'd never put a black fireman in because they'd have to sleep over and all. Finally, in April, Father O'Leary said, 'Deacon, we're havin' some meetings, but we don't want you in it; we want to do this ourselves.' I think it was right then that they called in Rudy Shields.

"I guess my position will always be misinterpreted. I told them, for God's sakes if there's a boycott, boycott me too. I'm sittin' in a ninety-per-cent-white neighborhood with ninety-per-cent-white business." He started thinking about closing his store until the boycott was over, because he was afraid people might assume he was after his own gain. "Then I got a threatening phone call. The only thing I hate is that some people might feel they made me close. Rudy Shields even offered to give me some bodyguards if I wanted to stay open.

"I closed the store for seven weeks. I was gettin' anxious whether if I ever opened up again I could make a livin'. So I talked to the mayor and found he was doing nothin', and the merchants association wasn't either, so I decided to open up again. Then the black people, thinkin' the white people had closed me down, flocked to me like long-lost friends. I closed to get Patenotte out of the center of things. I closed because I didn't want people to think I profited by the boycott. I closed so people would say maybe it's somethin' *else* bigger than Patenotte that caused this problem."

He estimates he lost nearly two-thirds of his white customers, but overall his business is 25 per cent better than before. "Before I had the richest people, and now most of 'em are on fifty- or sixty-dollar welfare checks." Suddenly he was silent. He scratched his neck and poured another coffee. "People try, you know," he said, looking over at me. "They really try. Some whites come into my store even now. They're fightin' against themselves. Some of these whites have been gallant. I understand. Believe me, I do. Friday and Saturday nights, when the blacks are here shoppin' with their welfare checks, some of the whites just feel squeezed out. I understand."

He had three young children enrolled in St. Clara's, the Catholic school. "They had three black kids goin' there. It was a rent-a-nigger situation. When school integration came, a whole group of new white children enrolled. They opened their arms to any child with twenty dollars a month, including a lot of non-Catholics. I resented this. I pulled my kids out of St. Clara's because I wasn't gonna give any segregationist an out."

The other day, Deacon ran into a black man in his store. The man started sending his children to the white school out at Benton a couple of years ago under the freedom-of-choice plan, and he told Deacon, "I had to move three times after I had freedom-of-choice."

"There's a big black man named Mr. Ingram. He told me just today, 'When I was a little boy, I had to walk three miles to school, and the bus full of white children would pass by me every day and never pick me up, even when it was rainin' or freezin', and I didn't understand why. I didn't understand till I was seven. Somebody asked me the other night what I thought of the school's integratin' in Yazoo, and I said *it's nice.*' "

Deacon said, "These youngsters ain't gonna allow that big ole bus to pass 'em by any more."

10

In the total school-age population of Yazoo, grades one through six have a heavy black majority; grade seven is the break-even point, after which the whites gradually become the majority. But the drain to the private school, even if not as large as the private school may have expected, had resulted in the blacks' outnumbering the whites right up through high school.

What of the young people? They are groping in pain and innocence toward something new, toward some blurred and previously unheeded awareness of themselves. They have suddenly found themselves growing up in a human situation fraught with nuances and possibilities they did not know existed before. The implications of this change in their lives, and the implications in the community itself, have hardly yet come to the surface. They are the first white and black children in America brought together under the courts' specific doctrine of massive integration, and they are intensely curious about each other. They fumble for words to express their new feelings. Black and white, they are children of the South, Southern to the core, and in this regard they are different from children in, say, New Rochelle or Los Angeles or Indianapolis. Yet like all young people in America, as Ralph Ellison suggests, "they have been unable to resist the movies, television, jazz, football, drum-majoretting, rock, comic strips, radio commercials, soap operas, book clubs, slang, and any of a thousand other expressions of our pluralistic and easily available popular culture." They are as American as they are Southern, but it is this common bond in the South —the rhythms and tempos, the ways of speaking and of remembering, the place and the land their people knew and out of which they suffered together—that makes them, young blacks and whites, more alike than dissimilar; and it is this, before it is all over, that will be their salvation.*

*Unlike the period from 1963 to 1965, when one could hardly pick up a magazine or a newspaper without reading of the region's latest barbarisms, there had by 1971 been very little written in the national journals of the South's move toward wholesale school integration. One of the notable exceptions was Marshall Frady's article in *Life* magazine, of February 12, 1971. "For all the violence and evasions since the Supreme Court's pronouncements in 1954," Frady wrote, "for all the continuing scattered incidents of rear-guard viciousness, what is under way in communities like Americus ... poses, even if flickeringly, the first authentic suggestion that it may be the South after all where the nation's general malaise of racial alienation first finds resolution. Not in the order of division prophesied by the old segregationists' apologists, but in the formal advent of a single people unique and richly dimensioned."

I had set up a meeting with a number of Negro students from the eleventh and twelfth grades the first week of the new semester. Several of them had gone to the white school for a semester under the token freedom-of-choice plan, but others had just come over from the Negro high school. At first they seemed shy, reluctant to talk in the presence of a white Mississippi adult, but after a time they warmed up to the prospect.

One of the girls said, "When we first got here, when they were by themselves they tried to be sort of friendly. But in a mass they were very standoffish. They didn't seem to know what to *do.* The poorer the kids, the less friendly they were. When they get by themselves with you, they talk about their family, their personal lives and all. I guess they think they can tell us everything and it won't get back to any whites.

"Some of the white girls try to be friendly, but I think they're a little bit scared. I sure do like the way they dress. Some of 'em are real cute."

Almost without exception, they said they had not made any "real friends" with white students, but one girl, who was the first Negro to integrate the white school two years ago, pointedly disagreed: "I have— well, not the type of friends who'd invite you to go ridin' around and go to parties and all that, but to talk about things. The first year I came over, I was just sittin' there. I'd be in a classroom but I wasn't part of it. People would talk all around me and ignore me. Now I feel more comfortable. They talk to me. I was in a physical-ed class and we were square-dancin'. Nobody wanted to hold hands with me, but a teacher put us in a circle and we held hands. When we went in the dressing room later, one of the white girls I'd been holdin' hands with went over to the sink and made a big show of washin' her hands. It didn't dawn on me for a while what she was doing. When it did, I went over and washed *my* hands.

"Things are better than they used to be. Now they'll walk beside you in the hall. They won't say, the way they used to, 'That nigger stinks.' In class some of the boys would open a window and say, 'I'm lettin' out some nigger air.' Every time I stand in a mixed line at the water fountain now, I can't help rememberin' my first year. I'd be standin' in line for water and they'd walk by and say, 'Don't drink that water, a nigger's been drinkin' there.'

"One day two white boys walked by me. One of them said, 'I smell a *gar.*' His friend said, 'What kind of gar, a ci-*gar?*' and the other said, 'No, a *Ni*-gar.' I couldn't help it. It was so crazy I just busted out laughin'."

Every one of them there had a story to tell, and they all started talking at once. "I think the younger black children will be able to get along with whites much easier," one of the boys said. "They don't feel inferior, not the way we did when we were children and things were different. Every day after school I see two little boys, one black and one white, headin' up Canal from the elementary school together. The black boy is ridin' a bicycle real slow, and the white boy is walkin' by his side. I've seen 'em every day."

"Some of the kids who came over this week," a girl said, "are complainin' that the school is like a prison. This school is more strict. We don't have as much freedom as before. There's not any social life at all. A white girl said to me today, 'You niggers thought you could chase us out. The only reason I came back was to show you we're not gonna run away from you.' I remember one of the white men said at the big meetin' that supported the public schools, 'We've got to stop runnin' away from these niggers.' "

Last semester five Negro girls went into the first meeting of the Y-Teens. "There were about twenty white girls in the room. They all talked nice, just as nice and friendly as you can believe. So word got out and the next week even more black girls came to the Y-Teens. After that the white girls didn't come back. I think they joined another club."

"One thing I find funny about the white students— they're always sayin' to me, 'Sirrinthia, what is *soul,* how do I get soul, Sirrinthia? What is soul music?' Or they say, 'How do you get your hair to stand *natural? Did you do it overnight?'* And they'll ask you to show them how to dance." Another of the students suggested that the whites aren't very good dancers.

"They try, though. They really want to. That's about the best way you can become friendly with them, when they ask how to dance, or what the top hits are, that sort of thing. Last semester they had their own radio program, and they'd always play black records, never any hillbilly. A boy in our class knows all the black hits. Sometimes I think they go home and memorize the lyrics and come back and sing to us. They say, 'We like the black hits, how come you don't like the white hits?' "

And another girl said: "When I was small I said I'd never live in Mississippi. Now I feel different. I want to come back, to help out a little bit." This drew a number of assents. One of the boys remarked that he had read about school integration in Little Rock. "We never had to go through all that."

11

I was invited to give a talk one morning to one of the brightest classes in the high school, a class of twenty whites and two blacks. From the first semester, only one out of twenty-three in the class had dropped out in favor of the private school. I turned the conversation to the school itself. When one of the Negro boys volunteered, "You can't have education if everybody opposes each other," several of his white classmates assented: *That's right. That's right.*

A white boy said, "It's gonna get more accepted as time goes by. The first reaction is the worst one. Nowadays we just have two schools in one building. It's like havin' two student bodies." "If the parents would leave us alone, we'd make it," another said. "They're much more upset than we are. We're gonna have to live with Negro people the rest of our lives. To tell you the truth, I kind of enjoy it. You certainly learn a lot about human relations. The parents are the worried ones."

Another boy, sitting right in the middle of the class, was obviously searching hard for words, for the beginnings of perception. "They're some white kids who think colored people aren't as good as whites," he said. "I know one white kid who went to the private school who thinks this, and you know . . . you know . . ." blurting out a conclusion, "he's not as good as Negroes. He's not as good as colored people!" *"That's the truth,"* someone shouted from the back.

There was one varsity basketball player in the room, a tall, pale white boy who had been silent through the whole class. The white team and the black team were just then having tryouts under the new integrated arrangement to choose a varsity, he said. "We clown around a lot together," he said. "It's real spirited and loose. We talk and congratulate each other. We'll be closer together now as a team than we were last semester."

Later that day, I met with a group of white student leaders, including two members of the student council and the editor of the paper. Alice DeCell, the editor and the daughter of the senator, was the leader of the group. She has organized this group, and I sense she is rather proud of her friends, that she has given considerable thought to her own reactions, and that she has discovered at the age of seventeen that to be a newspaper editor, no matter where, is to possess a strong responsibility indeed. She has performed this responsibility well, because time and again over the past year she has written editorials and stories touching deeply upon the considerations here that matter.

"A lot of the white students are indifferent, a lot are upset—only a minority are positively for it," Alice said. One white left just that day to go to the private school in Silver City. He said, "The niggers simply bother me. It just gets on my nerves to see 'em around." But one of the students, who calls himself a liberal on race, added, "The students have learned to respect each other's opinions. That's the key to it right now.

"Five years ago the people who were against integration—the rednecks—were in power both in the school and town. Now it's a little unfashionable to say you're against it. There's a generation gap here, just like everywhere else. People say it's the adult leaders who're makin' this work here, but I really think it's the students who've done it. I don't think the older generation here realizes how much the white people need the colored people." As a testimonial to the generation gap, several of the white students reported that the mayor has raised the restricted age from seventeen to eighteen for certain movies, and actually tried to stop the projector in the movie house during *Rosemary's Baby*.

They have disparaging words for the private school and its academic standards. The vast majority of the students there, they say, are girls. "The private school is a passing phase now. In five years they'll come back. A lot of the white students that stayed with our school didn't want to go to the private school, and they argued, and finally their parents just got tired of arguin'.

"The colored choir is very good. The white choir is terrible. People just aren't interested. So the white kids were kind of cuttin' up in choir the other day. The colored people were surprised, because they're serious about their choir. When the choirs came together the second day to see how we sounded together, I found that when the whites don't sing we're marvelous." They are full of complaints that all the weekly student-body assemblies, all the clubs, and the school social functions have been abolished by the authorities. They have two student-body presidents and two student councils "working in conjunction." Only athletics, the school band, the choir, and a few minor activities remain. The band was holding tryouts, and one of the girls said, "The band should be better. We need 'em like crazy. The colored majorettes look good, but I don't think the town will take *that*. It'll be interesting to see what happens when we elect the homecoming maids and the homecoming queen next year." The school yearbook, which normally does not go to press until the spring, was closed out in December. "No reason was given," one of the girls said, "but everybody knew why." "Who's Who," the school popularity contest which always is voted upon in the spring, was also held in December.

"The colored boys are exceptionally nice to me," one of the girls said. "They pick up my books if I drop 'em. One boy came up to me today and said, 'Hi.' I didn't know he was talking to me, so I didn't say anything. He said, 'Have they told you not even to talk to us?' I said no, I just didn't know you were talkin' to me, and he said, 'That's what they all say.' "

"Personally I'm more afraid of the girls than the boys," a white boy said. "The girls will say anything to you. The boys are a little scared, I think. But the boys seem to be going out of their way to be nice to you. I don't know if they're waitin' in ambush or really tryin' to be nice to you. Sometimes on the blackboards they write 'Malcolm X' and on their notebooks and their tennis shoes they write that African word, *'Shalom.'* In our first assembly, one of the colored boys said to a whole row of blacks, 'Be sweet and behave yourselves,' and then in a low whisper he said *'just so long as you act like niggers.'* They speak two languages. When they're talkin' to us, we can understand them. But when they talk among themselves, it's slurred and fast and everything. But what really amazes me is the number of colored kids who're so white. Some of 'em have pale skin and blue eyes. Sometimes it's pretty hard to tell." I am not sure he quite knew the reason why, however. Another of the girls said, "Some of the Negro girls are real neat.

They wear maxis and boots. Some of them really know how to dress. That Father O'Leary, he talks more like a white person than I do." And a boy added, "You don't expect a colored man to talk better than a white man. It's like expectin' to hear a dog talk, it surprises you so much to hear a colored person talk so good."

There is a book, Laurence Wylie's *Village in the Vaucluse,* which is a study of a provincial French town. The teen-agers there are like teen-agers every-where, and the writer describes in detail how they grow up and settle down and become the tight-lipped, hard-bitten, suspicious, long-enduring adults they are destined to be. This is the fall from grace, and it happens everywhere, but one leaves these children of Yazoo, its blacks and its whites, hoping for some ex-ception. There may be no exception forthcoming, but perhaps in the testing of their innocence together they will find, at the least, the possibility of a post-ponement.

It was now late in the afternoon, and as I drove down College Street near Firehouse Number 2, where my father used to sit with the firemen in his shirt-sleeves listening to Gordon McLendon's re-creations of major league baseball games, I noticed the lights were on in the high school gymnasium; the basket-ball team, the team from the two schools, had finished its tryouts. I parked the car and walked in-side, to look at the basketball court where I had played a hundred games, where Slick McCool roamed free and unacknowledged in the Delta Valley finals of 1952, where Bubba Barrier surprised us all that year by making eight points against West Tallahatchie, where I once sank a 20-foot jump shot as the buzzer sounded to beat Satartia. The scene of those vanished heroics seemed now quite deserted, and I stuck my head in the door. That basketball court was an echo in the heart, of all the odors of analgesic and tough-skin, and all the dreadful excitement, and the memories of all the boys who had toiled for glory here with me. *"Two, four, six, eight, who do we appreciate. Y-a-a-a-ZOO!"* The coach was giving a lecture to the new Yazoo High basketball team about keeping in shape, and that new team, sitting around him in a circle on the floor, consisted by my count of seven white boys and eight blacks.

I had the 9:23 to catch from Jackson, and I went by my house to say goodbye. "Don't be a traitor to your town," my mother said. "Don't hurt it. These are your people. You can't turn your back on us.

"It's cold now, but in another three months, just wait and see, it'll be green; remember how it was?"

12

March, 1970

I came back two months later, when the wildflowers and bushes, the vines and trees, were just beginning to show the wild disordered promise of the great Mississippi springtime. I had kept in touch by telephone; there had been one bomb scare, and a fist fight between a black girl and a white boy, but these had been the only serious incidents. After a few troubles (a teacher in study hall lost his temper at a Negro student, and all the blacks raised a commotion and gave the power clench), the white student president, Kenny Graeber, and the black president, Cobie Collins, gave speeches to the student body urging good manners. Ken and Cobie got identical letters from President Nixon praising them for encouraging "educational excellence." The NAACP had filed a contempt motion before the Fifth Circuit to completely integrate the classrooms, but it was apparent that such an order would not be made before the end of the semester. "The students have suffered a little from all this abnormal tension," one of the teachers told me, "but I think most of it's gone away." Everyone was a little tired, she said. "You can't wave a wand and create a new social environment. It takes a lot of hard routine work. There's no spirit of inspiration, which the school badly needs." But Bubba Mott editorialized in the *Herald* in March, under the title "Future Looking Good": "We perceive a distinct wave of optimism prevailing in this community. We believe the majority are aware Yazoo has weathered the worst of some adverse situations, which proved not as calamitous as one thought. Also there is a feeling that not only the worst is over, but that we are in an even better position to capitalize on the opportunities ahead."

More important, the white enrollment figures had remained reasonably firm. The public schools had lost seven hundred whites to the private schools since September. Harold "Hardwood" Kelley was still optimistic, and believed the white students who could not afford to keep paying the private tuition would gradually return to the public schools.

Rudy Shields struck a pessimistic posture. He was carrying a .38 up West Powell Street to the NAACP house when I cruised by in a car to meet him, and inside he put the pistol on his desk and complained about the segregation of classes and the demotion of all the black principals and assistants. "The black principals have only one function, and that's to discipline the black students. Black kids have to look up to *some* men in the schools, not just yes men. It's becoming apparent the whites don't want integration, and I'm not sure the blacks do now." Charles Evers and the other leaders would disagree with him, he said. "We tell our kids to try and get along and make friends but they haven't." In the last two months, however, he had seen a bright spot: "A few of the white and black students in high school are gettin' together and socializin'."

Ken Graeber, the white student-body president, star quarterback, forward, and shortstop who had been offered a golf scholarship to Ole Miss, came over from his house next door. He was a little boy the last summer I spent in town, and I took him around to watch baseball, and gave him dimes to ride the horses in front of the A. & P. He is now six feet two like all his brothers, and we talked about his father, Johnny, who used to sit with me on the porch in that dusty summer of 1956 and shout greetings at all the people riding by on Grand Avenue.

When the two high schools merged, the basketball team had to reschedule the rest of the season, and they couldn't get any games at such short notice. They had to wait until the Big Eight tournament started, where they played four games. "I get along fine with the athletes," Ken said. "If we could've played twelve games or so after integration, it would've had a good effect. We've always considered the athletes to be the leaders. We figured if we could show 'em it would work as a team, it would be a big help all over. I had to prove to the black kid that I was good enough to play with him, and he had to prove he was good enough to play with me.

"All of us were a little nervous at first. It wasn't dissension so much. Every now and then we'd get mad at each other, you know, when one of us was open and somebody didn't pass." In practice they had a Negro guard, a kind of Pistol Pete Maravich, on the team who threw behind his back and under his legs. "Once I passed a real good one to him behind my back, and he came up and gave me the soul-slap.

"I think basketball helped the town. People from other towns would come see us in the tournament because they'd heard about us and about these two big blacks we've got who could dunk the ball. Before the game the crowds would yell when we were practi-cin', *Dunk it, dunk it!*' "

13

The school paper had taken a random poll of black students, which had been censored by the paper's sponsor. Here is a sampling of what the blacks wrote:

People are finally realizing togetherness and acting to that effect.

It will only work if Black and White would work without malice toward none.

It won't be fair until classes are desegregated. It might as well be two schools again. I had hoped it would be different.

The atmosphere at YHS is dull and strained. The students are under strain as to whether to be friendly with the opposite race, which they want so badly to do, or to be hostile and aloft.

It will work if the people at the school would communicate more, and if they let that thing called prejudice be in the past. Because they can't all do much about it no way. I'm not speaking inteam of color people but with some of the white act as if it will hurt them to talk or even speak to the other young men or younger lady.

It will work just as soon as we realize, meaning both black and white students, that we were put here to love and live with one another, we will find that it wasn't as bad as we thought it was.

In the black students' classes you can count the no. of whites present in one or two counts, while in other classes the black students can be counted on one hand. I think the classes need to be desegregated on a ratio of 50 to 50. After this is accomplished the situation will be a success.

May YHS be in peace!

An editorial by one of the white students, Bruce Darby, was also not allowed to run in the *Yazooan*. It said:

Mississippians have witnessed the passing of an era. In a society traditionally closed to integration the crisis of desegregation has been met with reservations by many and passed in a frenzy of uncertainty. What Mississippi and Yazoo High School face now is an extended period of controlled progress.

The era of segregation has ended though not without noisy struggle and a new era has opened with new channels of racial communication and harmony.

The recent Federal Court order to desegregate 30 school districts in the state was the climax of many years of pressure to insure equal administration of federal and local programs without regard to race. The court order set off a vehement and very typical reaction on the part of most

Mississippians. Children were tossed into overnight institutions for the well-to-do citizenry of the state. They were thrown about excitedly as the white pieces in the game of chess in which the blacks had the advantage of national kings and queens. After a slough of overreactions came the final move. The white, playing the defensive, came back to surprise even itself with a change that thousands upon thousands of traditional white segregationists and resentful blacks will have to make in order for it to become a functioning reality.

We have been deluged with publicity from the instant outside evaluators. But we will not understand the full significance of what has taken place until we try to explain it to our children. . . .

In years to come Yazooans will increasingly appreciate the efforts of this generation. It will take patience, compassion, and empathy from all students at YHS to re-create the good school spirit that formerly existed in each of the separate schools.

We can do this by being courteous, by consciously trying to understand other viewpoints, by expecting cooperation rather than expecting resentment. It is a daily chore. Weeks of careful building of confidence can be dissipated in a rash moment of irritation.

We have a good start. Our basketball team worked together. Our chorus sounds great. Our student councils are communicating well with each other.

We think we can do it.

This time I talked with a larger group of the white students. They said there had been "fifty million rumors" going around town about white girls being molested, about fights and violence, and none of them were true. They were still dissatisfied with the way most of the extracurricular activities had been abolished. The most interesting area over the past several weeks, they reported, had been sports. During spring football practice, "a lot of black fathers came out and watched what was going on just like the white fathers do," and quite a few white and black parents turned out for the spring football game.

"The basketball players got to be great friends," one of the girls said. "They just loved each other. One night after a dance at the VFW, a bunch of us were foolin' around in front of Stop 'N Go, where the white kids always get together, and the white and black players went in together with their arms around each other like old friends. Then they all drove out to the country club, where there was another party. Everybody said, 'I can't believe what I'm seein'.'"

They were fascinated with the social life of the Negro students, who have big parties with bands on weekends for their various sororities and fraternities: the Tabs, the Betas, the Tab Sisters. One of the boys said he was with a white friend named Harley, who is somewhat conservative, and he proposed that they go to the Silver Slipper. "Harley said, 'That's a cool idea,' so we drove over there and were about to go in. 'Wait a second,' Harley said. 'I don't see any white people.' There was a colored boy standing out front, and Harley asked if a colored friend of ours named

Bozo was in the Slipper. The boy said yes and went and got Bozo. So Bozo came out and we talked, but that Harley never would go inside."

A few days before, the white and black student teachers had a meeting to talk about reorganizing student government: "One black girl said, 'We gotta have a *social.*' They really do want to get the two student bodies together. They want to start intramurals together and have a big social in the gym where everyone can get to know each other better."

One of the girls described an encounter with a black student named Clara. "Clara came up to me and said, 'Where you been? I haven't seen you in a week or two.'

" 'I've been right here in school,' I said.

" 'I don't know,' Clara said. 'I thought you gone to the private school and left me.'

" 'Oh, no. I haven't gone anywhere.'

" 'Well,' Clara said, 'you had me a little worried.' "

14

All through the Deep South, the towns which, by the spring of 1970, had been most successful in complying with the stepped-up integration orders were those where careful plans were made in advance and where reliable information won out over rumors. The lesson in Yazoo City and a number of other communities which largely stayed with their schools was that the majority of white Southerners preferred to integrate rather than see the public school system destroyed, and that economic considerations played a substantial part.* The organized efforts of these white leaders in Mississippi, Georgia, South Carolina, and Louisiana were often crucial in preventing the wholesale abandon-

*The March, 1970, issue of *South Today,* published by the Southern Regional Council, had the most reliable regionwide survey I have seen, and I am drawing on a number of their findings. See also W. F. Minor's "Mississippi Schools in Crisis," *New South,* Winter, 1970.

ment of the public schools during January and February of 1970. This was especially so in Mississippi, where the public schools in towns with ineffective and reactionary leadership were completely "resegregated" when most of the white students moved out to the segregated academies. In Mississippi as a whole, after three months of complete integration, the total public school enrollment in all the districts originally affected was down by about 15 per cent,* and in district after district in even the rural, economically backward areas, poor whites and blacks were going to school together. In Lawrence County's Monticello High, for instance, the reports read: tenth grade, 69 whites, 72 blacks; eleventh grade, 79 whites, 65 blacks; twelfth grade, 63 whites, 70 blacks. Silver Creek Elementary: fifth grade, 14 whites, 27 blacks; sixth grade, 13 whites, 24 blacks; seventh grade, 15 whites, 24 blacks. In a previously all-black junior high school in Jackson, now 45 per cent white, the PTA had reorganized and was half and half, and the white student president said, "To listen to some politicians talk, you'd believe it was chaos. There has been a minimum of any kind of friction. I think everything will work out fine. I believe in these kids." Even the most all-suffering reporters in Jackson were a little impressed. "It's like after a three-hundred-year common-law marriage,"

*Roughly one white student in every four left the public schools in early 1970. Some of these would return in the fall of 1970.

one said. "We're finally goin' to church to formalize the arrangement."

In Yazoo, the segregationist-academy people would argue with a considerable degree of optimism that when they completed their expensive new building, and if the classrooms were completely integrated in the fall of 1970, a continued drain away from the public schools would be inevitable, except among those who genuinely wanted their children to go to school with Negroes, under whatever circumstances, and among the very poor. Yet, as one Yazoo white suggested, there are really two distinct groups supporting the new private schools. One is the hard-core racists, whose absence from the public schools may in some ways be a blessing; the other is those who sincerely want quality private education. "And that is a built-in friction that's going to eat away at their innards," because you cannot have quality education buttressed by racism and an evangelical belief in exclusion. This observation would also hold true for the whole South.

No reasonable person in Mississippi believed that segregated public schools would ever come back; but among sophisticated black leaders deeply committed to integration the concern by the middle of 1970 was with *control* in the public schools.* With few excep-

---

*"In addition to the outright sale of school buildings, school boards gave a variety of other aid to private schools. In Forrest County, private school students rode public school buses. The Madison County school superintendent passed out a pre-Christmas

tions, wholly white school boards were still in charge, and it is they who set standards which amount to policy—segregated classes, as has been demonstrated, and various testing methods for teachers and students. Yet the idealistic spirit which prevailed in some quarters in Yazoo among whites and blacks was the national spirit of six or seven years ago. Black separatism was no more in vogue than recolonization to the Gold Coast, and despite their legendary deprivations, ninety-nine Mississippi blacks in a hundred would spurn the rhetoric of their own militants who would have them believe that integration was now passé, after all we had been through, and that one of the brighter hopes was the apocalypse in blood.

---

flyer telling students they could take their books with them to private schools. Amite County, Canton, and Yazoo County auctioned off school equipment including 'obsolete' desks and 'old unusable, broken and highly depreciated school desks, chairs, tables and lunchroom equipment.' The 'obsolete desks' went for 50 cents a piece. School buses were also up for sale. Although a new bus costs from $6,400 to $7,200, Canton sold a 1967 model for $250; in Yazoo County, a 1964 Chevrolet brought $126."—Luther Munford, *School Reformation,* unpublished Princeton thesis.

15

Less than one year after the integration of the first thirty Mississippi school districts, in late 1970, the effects of the *Alexander* decision had spread throughout the entire South. Those states which had been the most successful in adjusting to the change were those with enlightened leadership, from state governors on down. The Nixon Administration, which had done little to discourage the resignations of a number of key civil rights and education officials who had charged it with vacillation and bad faith (including several black administrators who said they could not face even the moderate black community after what the party of Lincoln was avoiding), claimed that by the end of 1970, 90 per cent of all black children in the South were in unitary school systems. Knowledgeable civil rights workers disputed that figure. Although many areas of the South had finally integrated their schools on a full scale with a remarkable absence of violence or ill will, the dual system in scores of school districts had not been abolished, and the goal of the *Alexander* decision was still far away. Indeed, the most direct and tangible example of the way the national Administration which ruled this disparate nation in 1970 had failed as any admirable guiding force was on just this matter. If the bedraggled and whipped-down New South were going to make it through all this, it would now be because of itself.

From all over the region during these early months of 1970, a number of the old-style segregationist leaders continued on the path of intransigence, re-enacting the old scenarios as if little had changed since 1954. The governors of Georgia, Alabama, and Mississippi were as defiant as ever. Even those school districts which had been predominantly or entirely abandoned to the blacks remained in the control of white superintendents and school boards, principals and athletic coaches in formerly all-black schools were being demoted, and black teachers were being fired.

Many school officials, local politicians, and conservative organizations followed the example of the diehard leaders.* The neighborhood school was their symbol, and they took an adamant stand against the use of free busing as a desirable method for ending segregation. Several techniques were used as the 1970

*Paul Gaston, "The South: Goal Still Distant, but Many Schools Go Well," *South Today,* December, 1970.

fall term opened to challenge the law. In Mobile, for instance, which had had a particularly long and exasperating history of defiance through the courts and where disillusioned young blacks came closer to talking the language of the Northern black extremists than anywhere else in the South (Roy Ennis of CORE had come there and had found a constituency among these hostile and pathetically disaffected blacks that was highly sympathetic to his idea of a separatist black state in Utah, Nevada, North Dakota, or southern Montana*), more than a thousand white students reported to schools to which they had not been assigned. The chairman of the Mobile school board called the integration plan which the courts had ordered "asinine" and said, "It's theirs and they can enforce it." In many integrated schools, a number of ploys were used to avoid the spirit of the law. A widespread use of "ability tracking" led to extreme situations such as the one in Franklinton, Louisiana,

---

*I was a delegate to a recent convention of "leading world intellectuals" at Princeton. Roy Ennis is a likable and engaging man, but when he stood up and expounded on his concept of the separate black nation in America (Africa-in-America was its name), the delegates from Europe and Asia were somewhat baffled, but largely took the idea seriously. Ennis spoke of a separate fiscal system, a separate foreign policy, a separate post office, etc. In the question period, a German philosopher was curious to know if the foreign policy would be linked to NATO and the Common Market, and an Italian sociologist inquired in some detail about the monetary issues.

Later a distinguished white American historian, a native of Arkansas, said, "Mr. Ennis, we tried that a hundred years ago and it didn't work."

in which 150 blacks were put in all-black classes and another 150 were assigned to classes with a handful of whites. In other schools, blacks were excluded from organizations and activities. And in most cases the whole stress of changing from one school to another was placed on black administrators and students.

By late 1970, there were an estimated 500 of the private segregationist academies in the South, and they were placing an immensely heavy burden on local economies, tax structures, and the very commitment itself to the notion of universal education. Many areas of the South had always devoted a more substantial share of their tax revenue to education than other parts of the country, and the cash drain of tuition payments that average about $500 a year per student threatened extreme damage to adequate tax support of the integrated public schools.

Most of the new schools were running on minimum budgets, and to make up the difference they went in for money-raising through carnivals, barbecues, entertainments, and cake sales. They sold brooms, dishpans, secondhand clothes, and trinkets which Sherman's deserters had failed to find even when digging up the ground in every last smokehouse in Georgia. Their faculties consisted largely of retired teachers and younger ones with questionable though highly dramatic credentials. Junie Brown of the Atlanta *Journal*, reporting on the private schools in

Georgia, found that many of them were more religious than academic, with preachers serving as headmasters and worship services consuming much of the day's activities. One private school in Athens gave courses in Bible, opened every morning with a religious assembly and prayer, ended each day with prayer, and intended to take its first graduating class to the Holy Land as a senior class trip. The headmaster of another academy said he opened his school because "I heard the call of the Lord."

Yet in Georgia itself no more than 55,000 children out of 1,100,000 had left the public schools, and the white exodus in other states was considerably below the expectations of the advocates of the private academies. In viewing the Southern schools as a whole in 1970, one could be cautiously optimistic despite some obvious and striking failures. One wondered if the more intelligent instincts of the region would somehow perceive just how inimical was the private school movement to the survival of the South as a vital, adaptable, and deeply communal society. For the races now had to get together to make the South, in its lasting promise to itself, the better part of the Great Republic, with lessons of no small consequence to the nation. And that the whites, or many of them, would have to learn.

"The peril," Marshall Frady would write as 1970 ended, "is that the impatience of blacks will constantly outstrip the pace of what whites regard as painful and substantial accommodations and accessions on their part. In the end, the real toll in the next few years of uncertain struggle will fall on the students themselves, both black and white, whose lot it could be to purchase, with their own patience and compassion and endurance and belief, the future of the South itself."

PART TWO

1

November, 1970

I was having dinner across from the state capitol with Bill Minor, the Mississippi correspondent for the New Orleans *Times-Picayune.* We had left the restaurant and were standing outside, in a cold and luminous November evening. Rain clouds were forming to the east, over the state office building decorated inexplicably with Kansas sunflowers, and as Minor talked he gestured in the direction of Mississippi's officialdom across the way, and to the clouds beyond. He is a sportily dressed man in his late forties, not as young as he looks, and what saves him from seeming dapper is that he is plainly a good old boy, but with reserves of intensity and no doubt contradiction beneath the boyish façade. He has been a journalist in Jackson for almost twenty-five years: his fellows both in and outside Mississippi regard him with an affection deriving not so much from seniority, although that would be sufficient, but from the

rare decency and fine humor with which he pursues
his calling, and the respect his own doggedness gives
to the profession of the working reporter, who seeks
no title more grandiose than just that. Many years ago
the old master, A. J. Liebling, wrote about him in a
"Wayward Press" column for some especially tenacious and courageous piece of work, and he has had
many offers to leave the state for better pay on one of
the big national papers. He does not want to go. To
him, Mississippi is one of the frontiers of our strivings as a people. He has despaired of its failings but
he knows, despite his experiences reporting its Em-
mett Till trials, its Neshoba County killings, its Jackson State shootings, and its more subtle defiances,
that it will survive as the last measure of its guilt and
travail. A couple of days before, a young white lawyer
in Greenville was entertaining some visiting English-
men who had come down to ascertain if Mississippi
did, as rumor had it, exist, and the lawyer had told
me, "They simply couldn't understand the emotional
investment we have in this place." Minor conjured up
for me now the young lawyer's remark. He will not
leave Mississippi because he has so much of himself
in it, in all its trials, hopes, and woes, and my guess
is that it takes a son of this outrageous and immeasur-
ably convoluted state to truly understand that.

"Listen. People who argue that the law can't
change a society are crazy," Minor is saying. "This
state is a perfect example of how law can change a

place. People down here are out in the bleachers. It's the federal law, the federal government, that's calling the real shots. The politicians down here like Maddox and Wallace and John Bell Williams think *they* are, but they're not. The changes that have been made in this state in the last few years have been astounding. And it's because of the federal law and the federal government. Even the Nixon Administration can't stop what's been started. All they can do is slow it down."

Bill Minor believed that the retreat among white children to the segregationist academies in Mississippi itself, with a much stronger private school movement than the rest of the South, had already reached its peak, and that a steady drift back to the public schools would be inevitable because of the high cost of those academies and because "it's already become socially acceptable among whites for their children to go to school with large groups of Negroes." He and his wife had a son in a school with a three-to-one black majority which had just elected a student body president "who is white, with long hair down to his shoulders." When whites complained of the possibility of busing, Minor would remind them that "they've been transporting children to school in Mississippi for forty years, ever since the internal combustion engine" and that the private academies in Jackson run by the Citizens Councils are busing *their* children, "and not only that, but in buses that are painted completely white." The Citizens Councils, which Hodding Carter once described as the Ku Klux Klan with a clipped mustache, existed now almost exclusively for running the segregationist academies, six of which were in Jackson.

There were those in Mississippi who would disagree with Bill Minor that the private schools there had "peaked," but now, on my sixth trip home in a year, in November of 1970, I found that ten months after Yazoo and the other school districts first underwent their massive integration, and three months after the other schools all over the state were affected by the *Alexander* decision of the Supreme Court, only slightly more than 40,000 children out of half a million in the state had dropped out of the public system. As one NAACP leader told me, "This is not a discouraging figure."

School integration was working best in towns such as Monticello and Aberdeen, with black populations ranging from 20 to 40 per cent. Even in Philadelphia in Neshoba County, which had become the bloodiest symbol of Mississippi racism during the vanished days of the Movement when the three civil rights workers had been murdered there, large-scale school integration was working extremely well. Its schools were the only two among the original thirty districts in the state to fully integrate their classrooms without court order. (The black school was closed down completely.) The little town of New Albany, William

Faulkner's birthplace in northeast Mississippi, had become something of a showcase. It completely desegregated its schools in 1969, and each school was now about 30 per cent black. The white parents reluctantly went along; now, out of 2,000 students, only two have gone to a private academy. As a result of testing, the black children gained 1.4 school grades in the first year of complete integration, and the whites 1.1 grades. But many of the counties in the heavily black areas of the delta had abandoned their schools to the blacks, as had the tier of heavily agricultural counties south of Vicksburg with black majorities. Jackson, the state capital, was perhaps the largest disaster of all; it could have been something of an example to the state. There 40 per cent of the whites left for the segregationist schools.*

In the midst of such basic change, there have been practically no violent incidents between black and white students from the high school level on down, even after the shootings at Jackson State in May of

---

*Mississippi has only four or five cities where there is any realistic possibility of public school busing. Most cities in the state are so small that busing would largely be a bogus issue, unlike other, more populous states in the South. In dozens of rural districts, children in Mississippi have always gone to school in buses anyway. In 1967, 58 per cent of Mississippi's students were bused to school, and the average bus route was forty-eight miles. Private Southern schools, in fact, bus students over considerably longer distances than public schools. In the few cities in Mississippi where busing might apply, it probably would be tolerated, as in Berkeley, California—integrated public schools to preserve segregated neighborhoods.

1970. For Mississippians, this was an amazing fact to ponder.* And the initial effort of the state to officially support the private schools by one method or another was no longer possible—not only because such a strategy was unconstitutional, but because too many state legislators had children in the public schools. Over twenty bills were introduced in the 1970 state legislature to help the private schools, but none was passed. The legislature rejected proposals to give tax credits up to $500 for donations to "educational programs" and to provide tax benefits on local school taxes to parents with children in private schools; nor was it receptive to the governor's plan to establish an elaborate organization of lawyers to infiltrate the North and expose its hypocrisy on integration.

Yet Mississippi had turned to the segregationist academies in proportionately greater numbers than any other Southern state. A white woman, the wife of a moderate state politician, told me: "You can't underestimate how all this has divided people—husbands and wives, children and parents, brothers and sisters, old friends." In white church groups and other organizations, another matron said, there has been "a lot of snootiness" on the part of parents of the private school students to those people whose children have stayed with the buffetings and uncertain-

*In February, 1970, 894 black students were arrested at Mississippi Valley State College and sent to Parchman, the state prison, for a night. They had been engaged in a peaceful demonstration and boycott. In 1969, there had been several fires in all-black schools.

ties of the public schools in this time of transition. In towns such as Senatobia in Tate County, the private school advocates exerted considerable pressure on white merchants to buy tickets to attend the large assortment of private school functions; this was undoubtedly true of many small towns throughout the state and the South. "The private school people," the Greenville lawyer told me, "are saying that all the tuition and building money and everything else are going right back into the local economy. Don't believe it for a minute. It's going right back into very restricted institutions." Two sentiments were foremost among the white moderates, and for that matter among many blacks. One was that the segregationist schools had badly overextended themselves and would be in grave financial trouble three or four years hence. The other was that many white children in the private schools wanted very badly to be in the public schools they had so recently left, but their parents would not let them.*

*William J. Simmons, leader of the Mississippi private school movement, argued that the percentage of whites who departed for private schools was "directly related" to the percentage of black students in the schools: "When integration up to 20–25 per cent takes place, a small number of whites leave, and the process continues until they separate into black public and white private schools." Others saw a clear tipping point at 50 per cent: "No district [of the first thirty to integrate] 50 per cent or more black lost less than 20 per cent of its white pupils. Two districts 48 per cent black lost only six per cent of their white pupils. The blackest district, Anguilla, lost 98 per cent of its white pupils. The whitest district, Forrest County, lost only 17 per cent but was an exception. The second whitest district, Neshoba County, lost only six per cent."—Luther Munford, *School Reformation.*

On this latter point, Winifred Green—who for years has been director of the Southeastern public education program for the American Friends Service Committee, and who has attained through her sheer knowledgeability and unswerving humanity the trust of almost everyone to the left of James O. Eastland from one oscillation in the national fashion on Southern civil rights to the next—was especially understanding. In the days I spent in Yazoo, I saw how removed were the private school children from the significant events taking place in their home town. Miss Green would speak eloquently of "the oppression of white students forced by their parents into the segregationist academies. It may seem strange to speak of children in schools designed to train them in the myth of their superiority as oppressed, but their isolation from reality can only mean that their choices about what they do with their lives will be limited. They may be a new generation condemned to live with all the guilt and self-deception that it takes to maintain the myth." Miss Green talked with a group of Mississippi high school students who had been taken out of the public schools early in 1970. "They didn't like their new school. They were confused and angry with their parents. They told the story of the history teacher opening the lecture on the Bill of Rights by making the offhand remark that 'he'd rather kill a nigger than sit at the table and eat with him.' "

The NAACP legal defense officials in Jackson were not so much concerned with the travails of these oppressed and privileged whites. They feared now that it would take at least another five years of litigation to carry out the latest court mandates. Enforcement was a major problem in 1970 because motions had to be filed in each separate case. Now that the United States Justice Department under John Mitchell had opted out of pressing most of the school and civil rights cases on behalf of the federal government, almost the entire legal burden rested with the plaintiffs. The NAACP people cited specific instances of discrimination against black children in integrated schools: in one town a black second-grader was spanked by a white teacher for kissing a white girl, and there had been other such examples. Practically without exception in the state, all the black principals have been demoted to assistants. Luther Munford reported that in Covington County a Negro principal who had a degree from Cornell was made "administrative assistant" in the new high school when his school became a junior high. The black high school principal in Leake County was made co-principal of the new high school, but was assigned to oversee the black side of the building. The black high school principal in Franklin County became an elementary principal. In Canton, the black football coach became "assistant principal for discipline" in the new high school and a white coach took over the predominantly black team. Fifteen per cent of the black teachers in the state who were teaching in 1969 did not have jobs in 1970. The NAACP was planning litigation on behalf of the demoted principals and athletic coaches and the teachers who had been dismissed,* as well as in the whole area of higher education in the state.

In some towns, there were the rudimentary beginnings of something that under the right circumstances could be portentous for Mississippi and the modern South: an alliance between poor whites and blacks centered on the public schools. It was much too early, in 1970, to give much credence to the short-range realities of such an alliance, but a division along class lines was certainly present in some places, and it would bear close watching. In places such as Sardis, a white politician told me, the lower-class whites had become extremely bitter toward the wealthier whites whose children had left the schools to a large black majority—a bitterness which could easily be translated into politics, such as school board elections. One of the most fascinating changes in the state had taken place in Indianola, a tough and recalcitrant delta town which was the birthplace, in the 1950s, of the White Citizens Councils. In Indianola in

---

*There was an ominous drift in the hiring of new teachers. When a black teacher leaves the system, a white usually replaces him. In 26 school districts in Mississippi, 800 new teachers were hired in 1970. Of these, only 158, or 19.7 per cent, were black.

January, 1970, the entire white student population had abandoned the public schools to 2,500 blacks. When the schools opened for the fall term of 1970, more than 200 whites had come back.* Some of the leaders in town discovered, after the whites' withdrawal to the private academy in January, that between 35 and 50 white children were enrolled in neither the public nor the private schools; they had merely dropped out unnoticed. Jack Harper, a lawyer, placed an ad in the local paper which said:

> There are those who say that we should forget about the whites ever using the public school system again. I cannot follow that line of thinking for many reasons. Among these is the undue financial burden that will be placed on the low and moderate income whites.

In the summer, a committee of the Chamber of Commerce took out another ad, pledging to work to maintain an atmosphere in the town "where parents, black and white, can send their children to the public school attendance center required by the federal district court, and where the teachers, black and white, may accept assignments to teach these children and retain their community status, dignity, and self-respect." Sixty people, including the mayor, several bankers, and businessmen, signed the ad. One 12-

---

*I have drawn on Ed Williams's excellent account, "Indianola: Why Whites Came Back to Schools," Greenville *Delta Democrat-Times,* September 6, 1970.

year-old white boy, who had returned to the public school, said, "I wanted to go back. We didn't go anywhere last time. Mama told us not to." He said he didn't mind being in the white minority. "We get along fine. The colored play better, too."

Jack Harper believed as many as 75 per cent of the whites would eventually return to the public schools in Indianola. The wealthy whites and the poor whites had their children in different schools with radically different philosophies; this amounted to a classic split along economic lines. "Do you think the whites and blacks in public schools are going to want school board members whose kids are in the private school?" one parent asked.

The picture in Mississippi remained blurred and unfocused, defying any easy generalizations. The rest of America had heard much about the relative peace and harmony in the town of Fayette, for instance, with its all-black government and Charles Evers as its mayor. Yet in the town itself, as well as in Jefferson County, there was not a single white enrolled in the public schools. And despite the remarkable strides which had been made in the state in such a short and critical period, there still was etched on the conscience of all enlightened Mississippians the reality of such places as Sunflower County, home of Senator Eastland, the county's largest landowner. Seventy per cent of the population are blacks, and they still live in what might be the worst squalor and poverty in America; there also the black children have the public schools all to themselves. On a statewide level, research done by civil rights groups had shown that out of the 270,698 blacks and 260,891 whites in public schools, about 100,000 blacks attend schools that are 90 per cent or more black, largely a result of the white withdrawal. In two or three places, there were notably discouraging setbacks. In Sharkey-Issaquena, which was 73 per cent black, an unusually large number of whites, led by a forceful newspaper editor, stayed with the public schools when they integrated in January, 1970. The example there had been more impressive than Yazoo City's, which has a somewhat smaller black population. But there was a fight between black and white students during the 1970 summer session, and in the fall many of the whites had transferred to the private schools.

Winifred Green, of the American Friends Committee, received a letter from the mother of the children who integrated the schools in Drew, Mississippi, in 1965, describing what was happening there in May, 1970:

The private school is going up here at Drew. Lord help these people. I wonder when people are going to learn people are people. Color don't have anything to do with it. There are some rich people and some poor people. Some able to eat, some can not. Some had a chance to go to school, some didn't. I can't understand why the U.S.A. care so much for people far away and don't care anything for people around them. They send money to help them way over seas. The U.S.A. is so crazy about them until they send our boys over there to die for them. Black boys, white boys. I can't understand this. Black boys in two wars, the one overseas and the one at Jackson State College. If we don't do what they want us to do and don't think like they want us to think they kill us. All we want is to be a citizen of the U.S.A. I am so fed up I had to put it on paper I guess. May the Lord bless us all.

2

But from the old surfaces, from the immemorial orders of life, something ironic and momentous was slowly emerging. An immense façade was beginning to crack, barely perceptible at first, but to a writer and a son of Mississippi, it was the little things which were gradually enclosing and symbolizing the promise and the magnitude of what might be taking place here. If a true human revolution implies the basic restructuring of everyday life, the essential patterns of behavior toward other people, then what might be occurring here was a revolution, subtle and intensely complicated. It would suggest itself in dozens of high school football stadiums on Indian summer Fridays in September, in those very towns where five years before the mere hint of a biracial council led to violence and mayhem and where now white adults sat in bleachers and cheered black fullbacks, white and black teammates exchanged soul-slaps after touchdowns, and black-and-white bands played

Sousa marches at half time. There would be traces of it in those countless scenes, repeated across the state as if they were molding into a kind of tableau, of small white and black children leaving their schools in late afternoons walking arm in arm along quiet deserted streets. Or in the white adolescents slipping off from home on autumn nights to the houses of black classmates to study their homework. This slow mutual awakening among the young across racial lines—in a place so condemned by its fellow countrymen, and indeed some among its own people, that it seemed to suffer from the very blood curse itself, which D. W. Brogan as recently as the mid-1960s called "the most savage and backward of all the American commonwealths"—was a small affirmation of the heart.

One Friday night in the town of Leland, where the public schools are 80 per cent black, the leading white plantation owner and banker accompanied his yardman—a black who has worked with him for years, cutting his lawn and clipping his hedges—to the high school football game. They sat in the grandstand together to watch the black yardman's son, who is the starting quarterback.

A photograph in the Greenville paper showed the football homecoming court for the high school: six black girls and two white, and they were all smiling.

Several photographs in the Jackson papers were of white and black mothers, in almost equal numbers, conferring on the business of the schools their children attended.

In one delta town where the black and white high schools and their football teams merged, the Rosedale Bulldogs and the Rosedale Vikings were now the Rosedale Eagles, and the new team colors were red, white, and blue.

At a basketball game in southern Mississippi, a drunk white man actually shouted the lines to an archaic joke when a black from his team got into a fight with a black from another team: "Get that nigger off our *Nee*-gro!"

The University of Mississippi, the campus where the riots occurred when James Meredith was admitted in 1962, had a High School Day and invited students to come and look around. Hundreds of young blacks accepted the invitation. At the Ole Miss–Houston football game on the same day, a group of blacks unfurled a sign in the bleachers which said, "OLE MISS EQUALS RACISM." But when the Ole Miss quarterback, Archie Manning, broke his arm and was helped off the field, the same blacks who carried the banner were suddenly silent, then applauded him.

A white politician said: "After what I've seen in the last few months, I think Mississippi could become the most liberal of all the Southern states."

A white woman said: "I'll say this, they sure are gettin' *cleaner.*"

An industrial plant opened in the town of Heidelberg. Dozens of blacks and whites shook hands, drank coffee, and talked together in a cordial atmosphere. Off to one side as the guardian of law and order was a black deputy sheriff with a gun in his holster.

At a school in Jackson, the black and white students asked for permission to have a dance together. The black principal conferred with several mothers and decided to go ahead. The central school office vetoed the idea.

Two white men were talking over the prospect of black governments in several counties. One of them said to the other: "Before too very long you're gonna get a call from a black sheriff tellin' you, 'Boy, you better come on down here and pay your taxes.'"

The daughter of a white woman went to an interracial convention, and when she got home she received a letter from a black boy. "What do you do about this when you're the girl's mother?" the woman asked. "Where will all this lead? Can you tell me that?"

3

November 15, 1970

In Jackson, the town where I was born, there were decals of American flags now on hundreds of cars. There were more flags of the Grand Old Union on moving vehicles than I had seen on taxicabs in Brooklyn, or for that matter on hard-hats in Manhattan. I was baffled, remembering that back during the halcyon days of the Movement the American flag had been the symbol of the integrationist reformers, Yankee outsiders and Southerners alike, and the segregationists sported the Confederate flag, and often stooped to meaner things in the very name of it. After a time, one can almost *sense* a seg car when he sees one, and these were now proudly displaying the Stars and Stripes. I asked a young lady whose political opinion I trusted in Jackson why this was so. "They think the rest of America has changed its mind," she said.

The old town was different. The splendid nineteenth-century houses on North State Street were

gone, replaced by insurance firms and service sta-
tions and a luxury Hilton. A friend and I drove by a
gigantic new shopping center, the largest I had ever
seen, with more shoppers than the Federals had foot-
soldiers when they marched from Vicksburg in 1863
and burned down much of the town. "It's sure not the
Old Confederacy," my companion remarked. Later I
drove by the place where my grandfather Percy once
made potato chips, back in the 1940s, and then over
to North Jefferson Street; the little brick house at 1017
North Jefferson where I spent the summers of my
boyhood, where Percy and my grandmother Mamie
sat on the front porch on hot windless summer evenings greeting the people out for walks, was now a
parking lot for the Jitney Jungle across the street. The
magnolia tree I used to climb now shaded the parking
lot, and I found a couple of rusty nails I had ham-
mered into it a quarter of a century ago to build a tree
house, a roosting place not too far up among the blos-
soms where I could be a sniper against the Japs once
they captured Jackson. I looked around for myself
there that day—I really did: for a small lively boy, a
little smart-assed but kind to old women and to stray
dogs and the colored as he had been taught, in a
Brooklyn baseball cap and sneakers and short blue-
jean pants torn off at the bottom, but he was as gone
as the house was. The absence of the old house itself
brought a mournful hymn to my heart, and I went to
the bar of the Sun 'N Sand for a drink, where I over-

heard a woman say to her three male companions, "I never had a Yankee lover. Are they any different?"

On Capitol Street, they were building an enormously high brick wall all the way around the Governor's Mansion, thus blocking from view the most gracious and beautiful ante-bellum home in the city. It was in this Mansion that my great-grandmother and great-grandfather first met before the Civil War when my great-great-uncle was governor, and for years it had stood there in the center of town for all to see and admire. The wall, with the guardhouses built into it, was the idea of the present governor, John Bell Williams, and I later learned that it caused much controversy and agitation. It was being built at a cost of $133,000 to provide the governor with privacy and protection. "It's a fitting monument to John Bell Williams," one unregenerate cynic in the legislature said. "He'd build a wall around the whole state if he could get away with it, and just toss people he didn't want over into Alabama, except Wallace would toss 'em right back." The governor told friends he was building the wall because people keep crawling off the street into the bushes around the Mansion to sober up. The same cynic told me, "I think the problem is more people are crawlin' out of the Mansion than crawlin' in."

I had come here to Jackson to give a lecture at Millsaps College, a predominantly white Methodist

school, with Ralph Ellison. I was supposed to meet
Ellison at the airport, because I was coming in from
Dallas and he from New York, but we got our days
confused and I was not there to greet him. Instead a
news commentator from the big Jackson television
station, a station which has gone through a lengthy
round with the Federal Communications Commission over racism in its programing, recognized him
and gave him a lift into town. The price of the ride,
however, was that the news commentator persuaded
Ellison to go to the TV station with him, where he
interviewed Ellison for half an hour. After an infor-
mal discussion at the college (where a white adult
complained that "the colored folks are robbing
graves in Kemper County"), Ellison and I strolled out
into the porch of the cafeteria, into a luxurious afternoon. Students were hurrying along the shaded path-
ways of the campus to class, and under an oak tree a
few feet away three young blacks, books under their
arms, paused for a moment in muted conversation.
Suddenly, having caught sight of Ellison gazing
across the campus, they were quiet and still. They
stood there, dark silhouettes against the bright sun,
looking him over from head to toe. He must have
sensed their stare, for now he looked their way, and
for a slight flickering moment across that small distance their eyes met—in what?—recognition? curiosity? irony? Ellison smiled very slightly and looked
down at the grass, lightly kicking the earth with the

toe of his shoe. The young blacks exchanged a brief glance among themselves, then strolled away.

The joint lecture was a success, and then there was a party in the house of a professor of religion, with a large group of black political leaders there, as well as several of the Jackson press corps. Most working reporters are always several leaps ahead of the places in which they earn their keep—after a time they see through the official posturing and the defensive rhetoric—and this group was no exception. To a man they struck me as intelligent and reasonable, and they spoke of the state, as Bill Minor had, with a realistic understanding and an affection unencumbered by fanciful expectations or sham idealism. When they talked of the strange things taking place in Mississippi, they did so with much relish and humor, and perhaps even a little awe. It was no surprise that they were drawn immediately to Ellison, who described to them his travels across America on the lecture circuit and his growing up in Oklahoma, for great novelists to working reporters are the ultimate of the craft. Ellison and Eudora Welty talked for a while: Where had they first met? "In Harlem in April of 1940?" asked Ralph. "No, it was *May*," replied Eudora. Back at the motel, several of us sat on the balcony, drank bourbon, and watched the rain dripping off the leaves, advising a young white college student from New York City who had come down to decide whether to attend Tougaloo College for a year that he ought to do it. "*Try* yourself," someone said. "It's a mighty good time to be here." Ellison later said he returned to New York and told people the state of Mississippi was getting different, but no one very much believed him.

Two or three days later, I spoke to an audience of "white moderates" at the Old Capitol, having been asked to talk on New York, on writing, and on my home town. One hoped that no Mississippi governor would build a wall around that splendid building, which dated to the 1830s and now, in its tastefully restored condition, a revered hall much face-lifted and serene, dominated Capitol Street and the hills below. The speech was in the chamber of the old Mississippi house of representatives; in this chamber my uncle gave many of his exuberant orations as governor in the 1850s; the state of Mississippi seceded from the Union in this room in December, 1860; and when my great-grandfather was a member of the legislature, my grandmother Mamie, as a very little girl, would come to town from Raymond to sit in his chair on the house floor and hear him speak. I was aware in this chamber of the ghosts of my people: what they had said and done in this room, where they had triumphed and where they had failed, and the destinies of the cause that had most reluctantly been in their hands. Old friends were there from Yazoo, including Bubba Barrier and "Red" Wallace, All-Conference blocking back for the Yazoo Indians when I

was a boy; Barbara Nell Hollowell, one of the finest of
the double-named belles who had shared the Yazoo
days and consoled us in many Delta Valley Conference defeats; Rosemary Thompson, who had taught
us to read Shakespeare and to parse a sentence; and
Laurie Stigler, a one-time editor of the now defunct
but still proudly remembered Yazoo High *Flashlight.*
Afterward a young white high school student, a
skinny red-haired boy in a pullover sweater, introduced himself to me as the president of the senior
class in a small Mississippi town; then he corrected
himself, saying, "No, I'm the *co*-president." His
school was 50 per cent black and 50 per cent white, he
told me, "and we're gettin' along just fine, just *better*
than fine," adding a little wistfully, just as my grandmother had a few months before, "If only folks will
let us alone to grow."

Mel Leventhal is the main school lawyer for the
NAACP Legal Defense Fund; it was he who argued in
early 1970 that the classroom segregation within the
integrated school buildings, in Yazoo and elsewhere,
"is just as debasing as before." Leventhal is 28 years
old, a Jewish boy from Brooklyn, and a graduate of
the N.Y.U. Law School, but he speaks in a Southern
accent, with only traces of the Big Cave's sharpness,
and he expresses a strong love for Mississippi and
believes it someday could become a "great state." He
is a large man with open features who uses the word

"fella" when talking to you, much as a Kappa Alpha during rush week at Ole Miss would. But he is tough —and smart, a shrewd smartness curiously mingled with a kind of latter-day Southern gentility; as a student in New York, he spent considerable time at the race track. Once, he and I had been sitting in a beer-drinking place called the Mayflower on Capitol Street late on a Saturday night, with country hard-noses at the bar drinking Jax while Johnny Cash advised them from the jukebox that flesh and blood ought to get together now and again. A young white man at the next table had been eavesdropping, and as he walked over to where we were sitting I thought, with the unerring reflex of all my growing up here and the hard jangling late-Saturday mood of the place, This is trouble for sure. But the young white man turned out to be the lawyer for the school board in a little town further south that had just integrated its schools. He and Leventhal were on opposite sides in some litigation then pending, and he said he wanted to meet Leventhal, and he extended his hand and joined us in the talk. This, also, would not have happened five years before, at least not in public on a Saturday night.

I had arranged to meet Leventhal at his office on Farrish Street, where he is in partnership with several Negro lawyers, and we drove to his house in a black neighborhood for dinner. His wife is a black from Georgia, a graduate of Sarah Lawrence, and a novelist who writes under the name Alice Walker. Her parents were sharecroppers in a small town, and she had been one of half a dozen children. She had just had a magazine piece accepted for publication in a Southern journal and she had given it the title "The Black Writer and the Southern Experience":

What the black Southern writer inherits as a natural right is a *sense of community.* Something simple, but surprisingly hard, especially these days, to come by.

In large measure, black Southern writers owe their clarity of vision to parents who refused to diminish themselves as human beings by succumbing to racism.

. . . Southern black writers, like most writers, have a heritage of love and hate, but they also have enormous richness and beauty to draw from. And having been placed, as Camus says, "halfway between misery and the sun," they, too, know that "though all is not well under the sun, history is not everything."

No one would wish for a more advantageous heritage than that bequeathed to the black writer in the South: a compassion for the earth, a trust in humanity beyond our knowledge of evil, and an abiding love of justice. We inherit a great responsibility as well, for we must give voice to centuries not only of silent bitterness and hate but also of neighborly kindness and sustaining love.

"I sometimes wonder if integration is really worth the effort," she is saying. She believes in the children working it out together, but worries if all the pressures on them now might finally prove destructive. We were sitting at the dinner table, with their year-old daughter in a highchair. "The two of us took her into Sears the other day," Mel Leventhal said. "Everyone gathered around and looked. It almost caused a riot." (I thought, Who would take on the likelihood of a mulatto child, and in Mississippi, unless both were exceedingly strong and were trying hard to redeem themselves?) The talk now is about the South, of the land itself—"Can you imagine what the delta must have been like a million years ago?" she says—and of what might come out of this time of critical change. Her husband believes school integration itself will succeed: "But I'm not at all optimistic that we'll have one society. And what worries me is that if we're not going to have one society, school integration may not be worth it."

His wife Alice is strikingly beautiful, a quiet and sensitive girl, a little different, who grew impatient with the East when she was a student there, and whose heroine is Flannery O'Connor. She is a Southerner—and in fact reminds me a little of myself—but I doubt if she gets out of the house very much in Jackson. I know that despite her husband's highly active life as the lawyer for blacks, they are ultimately quite private and alone. "Sometimes it gets to you, the pressure," he said. "Going to a movie together. Holding hands walking down the street." We were standing at the doorway as I was about to say good night. "I think you wish you'd never left Mississippi," she is saying. "The more I hear you, the more I believe you really want to live here."

Here in Mississippi? *To live and die in Dixie?* Just
that afternoon, killing a little time sitting in front of
the state capitol on the steps of the monument to the
Women of the Confederacy—a squat, ugly blocklike
structure extolling the virtues of its mothers, sisters,
wives, daughters, aunts, cousins, and grandmothers:
a tempestuously rhetorical memorial which would
make the most belligerent and sharp-elbowed
women's liberationist in New York circa 1970 blush
with envy—I pondered the question of geography,
wondered at its rather predictable complexity, and
asked if it really meant anything any more.

That morning, I had gone with my mother to the
nursing home near Raymond, the old family home
town, to see again my grandmother Mamie, whom we
had put there several months before. Sitting now in
the room she shares with the paralyzed old woman
who has no people, no forebears, no children, who
shouts and pleads for someone to come fetch her
away, as if she senses in her mad and terrible decline
some immemorial wrong has been done her by tangible living flesh, Mamie spends her days in complete
blindness, oblivious to her roommate's cries, speaking only to herself, in half-mumbled ruminations, of
the past. Percy, Mag, Sue, Ella, Mama, Papa . . . she
endlessly talks to them as before, plotting in small
detail the events of Sunday afternoons in 1885, or
1898, or 1904, expecting someone long dead to arrive
now at any moment, holding in her tenacious remem-

brance her ineluctable loves and carings. Her skin is dry and wrinkled as parchment, and she is tiny like a toy, living in an impenetrable darkness, sitting now only a mile or two from where she once was a girl, where her husband Percy proposed to her on the improbably steep and rounded wooden bridge over the railroad tracks at the depot where the finest trains in Mississippi once stopped, where she studied through three or four school grades in an old house now owned by people from Jackson, where she buried her mother and father and brothers and sisters and cousins in the old part of the cemetery now overgrown with brush and weeds.

"This is your grandson," my mother is saying loudly, touching her on the arm, shaking her a little. "Do you remember your grandson?" The old woman in the next bed, her arms no rounder than cucumbers, shouts *Grandson, Grandson!* and Mamie says, "Who? . . . Percy? Sam? Winter? Marion?" *"Your grandson!"* my mother persists. "Here from New *Yawk*. You haven't seen him since he and your *great*-grandson David came from New Yawk together. Remember? His hair was longer than Jesus Christ's. *Remember, Mamie?"* Now something touches her face, a brief suggestion of some buried mirth, and she strains against these old burdens of time. I can almost feel her struggling against them, as one summons all his reserves to surmount the edge of some unconquerable and final precipice: and then, with a sudden movement of her eyes and the puckish grin I remembered from my childhood, she says: "Sho 'nuff? Is that *boy* really here? All the way from New *Yawk?* Let me feel his hand. When that boy was little, he was always up to *somethin'*." Then she has gone from us again.

Now, a few hours later, sitting on the steps of the monument to the Women, I am watching the comings and goings of the Baptists, who are meeting in state convention assembled across the street at the First Baptist Church, strolling in clusters across the capitol grounds with an air of such sweet and satiated and omnipotent piety that my Methodist wellsprings turn a little sour. Two small Negro children walk past, pointing upward at the spreading magnolias which never lose their leaves even in the winter. Do you think they sense, these are *our* magnolias now too? If a certain era began in 1956, when Rosa Parks refused to give up her seat on a bus in Montgomery, then it ended here in front of this state capitol ten years later, in 1966, when an assemblage of Negroes, continuing the wounded Meredith's march down a highway south of Memphis, first raised the cry of black power. But that too is only transitory, marking a time when new complications set in and the predictably noble gave way to a demonology of good and evil: I am aware now as almost never before that all my people who founded and nurtured and then led this state and suffered themselves its worst calamities are buried under vanished or broken tombstones in the gutted and overgrown graveyard ten miles away, that my great-grandfather met my great-grandmother in the Mansion enclosed by the half-finished walls and guardhouses two blocks across town, that my great-uncle thundered his rhetoric in the tiny chamber of the restored building up the street, that my grandmother Mamie waits in blindness in the nursing home down the road, that the house where I spent my summers as a boy is now a parking lot for the Jitney Jungle—and that I, the inheritor of all this, can hardly bear its burdens, am *in misery with the past,* and yearn for 9:23 A.M. day after tomorrow, when the plane will once again take me back to the cultural capital, the Big Cave, to its inchoate rootlessness and security.

4

November 16, 1970

Yazoo again. "The mimosa tree is turning Daddy upside down," my mother said.

But I had already found that out. The first thing I had done when I got there from Jackson this time, in a still and wonderful November twilight in a rented Hertz, was to drive once more into the cemetery to his grave. For the cemetery had always been the most beautiful place in town for me, and in some ways the most sensible; I have always walked among the new gravestones to see who had died since the last time I was here, knowing that if I do not find them here I will probably see them drinking coffee at Danrie's, or in front of the Bon-Ton or the Delta National Bank. The tree, which we had planted the day after my father was buried and which at first seemed as sickly as the sorriest pup in a litter, had put its roots deeply into the ground, tilting the gravestone at an angle and

151

digging up the earth around it. So it was at an angle that I read the inscription on the tiny stone:

Henry Rae Morris
Tennessee
PVT STU Army
TNG Corps
Jan. 8, 1899   Sept. 2, 1958

I stood alone on the hill where he is buried, hearing the lonely echoing whistle of a late-afternoon Illinois Central down below in the town, and the same old barks of the delta dogs who have always seemed to become alive or horny or simply communicative in this dying hour. All around his grave on the hill were the graves of his friends the American Legionnaires who sponsored and coached our championship baseball teams when I was a boy: Herman Nolte, "Red" Hester, Charlie White, Sammy Moses, whose son is now catcher with the California Angels, and all the others. We buried him here two days after I was married, my wife and I making a maddening trip against time from a honeymoon on one of Lyndon Johnson's artificial lakes somewhere in Texas: the police chief, Mr. Ardis Russell, had stood at attention with his cap on his heart as the hearse made its way through the streets of the town; the firemen, domino players, hunters, and fishermen mourned him the most; and I was sorry I had not told him, the last time I saw him in the hospital before I went off to Texas to get married, that if I ever had a son I would give him his name. He had made a baseball player out of me, and had taught me to hunt. When the time had come for me to go to college, he had traveled five hundred miles on a Southern Trailways bus to look over the University of Texas, and when I telephoned him one cold December night in 1955 from New Orleans to say I had won a Rhodes scholarship, he had said, for he was a simple man, "Boy, you'll never have to worry about a good job the rest of your life." He was making fifty dollars a week when he died.

Twelve years had passed since he was buried and we planted this indefatigable mimosa tree. My marriage was gone, and I had become a member of the New York literati. Sorrow had embraced me like a small madness. It had settled into my taste buds, and had a territorial stake in my gonads. Overnight, so it seemed, I lost not just a wife who had been my college sweetheart, but also a New York apartment, all my books, an old farmhouse with six acres on a hill, and my 85-pound black Labrador retriever named I. H. Crane—as fine a dog as I ever had; I loved to watch his big old ears flopping in a summer's wind, the way he rooted around in the snow and humped the leg of the table in the kitchen and jumped over waves in the ocean—*lost!* I remembered Christmases in the farmhouse with the eighteenth-century beams, a yule log in the fireplace like the fireplace in Patrick Henry's kitchen, an evergreen high as the ceiling: my six acres, my books, and my old dog I.H. But all that was far behind; I was now the age my father was when I was born, and his grandson David Rae spoke with a Yankee accent and had developed an interest in ice hockey. *"Ice hockey!"* he would have said. "Where do they get the ice to play it on?" Because he was a simple man who loved this town, I wondered what he would think of the changes that had been made here in these twelve years. "The niggers pay taxes, don't they?" I once heard him say when I was a child. "If they pay taxes, they have the right to vote. It's just that simple." It was the first such thought I believe I ever heard, the first that was different from what I had been used to, and my guess is he would be proud of the town now, and would see crucial days ahead.

I was driving out of the cemetery down Canal Street. I saw fifteen or twenty black youngsters crossing the lawn of my old high school, books in hand, heading for home; my mind was back again to twenty years ago. As they left Yazoo High School and walked up the white street, the Negro kids were shouting and laughing and throwing things at each other. I drove past them, and slowed the Hertz down and stared. A couple of them caught my stare and looked right back. In a few seconds they were all staring at me. "Hey, man," one shouted. "What you think you *lookin'* at?" For the first time in a year, the thought struck me, hit this exile a reeling blow, My God, they aren't what they used to be. What have they done to my old school? Too much of my past welled up within me from this isolated delta town where they once were *ours,* existing at our whims and mercies; too much of my growing up was still with me.

Chewing-Gum Smith and Mr. Dement Warren had also just died: Chewing-Gum Smith, who drove the American Steam Laundry truck and managed the semi-pro baseball team, once throwing a Louisville Slugger baseball bat into the grandstand as a gesture of his extreme disaffection when I was called out in a slide at home plate, then being ejected from the game and watching the rest of it crouched on his heels in a cotton patch, wagging his head and chewing furiously on his gum; Mr. Dement Warren, who ran the men's-clothing store at Main and Jefferson, whose apparition I saw all over Manhattan the first day I moved there, for my psyche must have succumbed out of Manhattan's awesome present to my half-remembered past, and of whom a friend would say on the day he died: "Mr. Dement spent almost all his life here, and yet he's bein' buried in the town where he was born. It's a cryin' shame. Mr. Dement belongs *here.*" As my high school English teacher once told me, "Death in a small town is like death in no other place." Imperceptibly, in a few short years, one generation in Yazoo had given way to the next. And what of the one after that?

A small catalogue out of the life of the mimosa tree:

The black economic boycott had ended on September 1, 1970. Rudy Shields had left town to do organizational work elsewhere, and when Father O'Leary again became the black leader, his first act had been to negotiate an end to the stalemate. Business was better, and some of the town leaders were arguing for an ambitious urban renewal program that would change Main Street to a luxurious shopping mall without cars.

The high school football season had come and gone. There had been six blacks on the team, which played before sizable crowds of black and white adults. Larry Kramer, the star halfback who Jeppie Barbour, the mayor, had said would insure an abiding community interest in football despite the integration, had made the All-American high school team.

The ratio of blacks to whites in the public schools, slightly less than a year after complete integration, had decreased somewhat, with some 140 whites out of slightly more than 700 coming back from the private school, not a negligible percentage. About fifteen whites from a separate school district in the county, in fact, were paying $285 a year tuition for the privilege of attending the public school. The only incident had been a fight between two blacks in the study hall at the high school, and the principal told students there had been less trouble than any year he had been on the job. "There is a little less anxiety, less of the unknown," a teacher said. "We're not nearly so self-conscious as we were last year. The school just sort of operates in an unusual normal way."

The new private school building, the Manchester Academy, was almost completed, on the very cotton patch across from the old baseball field where Chewing-Gum Smith had squatted on his heels and watched the baseball game after he was thrown out. When the Manchester Mavericks were playing another segregationist academy, the Sharkey-Issaquena Rebels, one black student in Yazoo High School told some whites, "I think I'm gonna go over there in blue jeans and a T-shirt, barefoot and carryin' a Confederate flag, and see if they'll let me in." A group of white students went to the game and sat on the other side of the field cheering for the other team. There had been a continuing dissatisfaction among some of the whites in the private school. "I hate Manchester as much as I do niggers," one of them said. A white student leader in the high school told me, "I doubt there will be much of a Manchester five years from now. Even the private school people are more tolerant now. They know it's too late to fight it. We're gonna have a normal integrated public school. It's even more normal now than it was last year. And the children in elementary school by the time they get to high school will be so used to it." A white girl, overhearing this, said, "Why, just yesterday, a black boy who sits behind me in homeroom asked my advice on his problems with his girl friend." A friend of hers said, "I was readin' *Black Boy,* by Richard Wright, and a black sitting next to me leaned over and looked at the book and asked, 'Why you readin' that?' 'Because I like it,' I said. 'Really?' he said. He seemed amazed."

In the senior class at Yazoo High, the election for class president between a white boy and black boy ended in a tie, 100 to 100, so there would be co-presidents. The sophomore class elected all-black officers. In the junior class, which consisted of 132 blacks and 118 whites, one white boy was running against four blacks for class president. The white candidate got 116 votes; the black vote was divided. "The blacks got the hang of it," a white student explained. "All the blacks except one dropped out, and the main black candidate won by 130 to 118." His name is "Gentle Ben" Williams; he is the son of a maid.

There was no distinct segregation now in the classes. The ratio of black teachers to white in the high school, for instance, was running about 45 to 55, and the blacks were teaching classes just as mixed as the whites. There were ten American history classes in the high school, each of which were close to half and half, but in some courses such as English and arithmetic, grouping was based on achievement tests. The top group here was only about 15 per cent black, and the middle levels were mixed. Every grade from the seventh through the twelfth had at least one all-black "remedial" class, however. "They're so far down, unfortunately, they should be in special education," a teacher said. "Of course, why they *are* so far down is another question."

Almost all the school activities and clubs had remained out of school. The newspaper, the *Yazooan,* had a sizable black representation, and so did the yearbook. The basketball team was predominantly black, but the cheerleaders, elected by the football team and the student council, have all been white. For the homecoming football game, one white girl and one black girl were elected the official queens by secret ballot from each class. There was a parade down Main Street, with a black girl and a white girl in each convertible—a juxtapositon which caused certain tremors between town and gown, for this, among other things, was quite clearly unprecedented, and had taken place far removed from the protected sanction of school property. The town survived it, as it likely would other new precedents in future years, whatever they might be. The white high school students had had dances, but their black classmates were not invited, although, as one white girl said, "They've certainly invited us to theirs." Many of the homerooms have an occasional party in the school. At one of them, the students took turns playing "black" and "white" records. The band director, a kindly gentleman named Stanley Beers, who many years ago taught me to blow a loud and faltering trumpet, refused to play "Dixie" at the football pep rallies. "We did play 'Dixie' at the last home football game," a member of the band said, "but when we played it, it sounded more like a hymn than a fight song." The blacks in the band are mainly drummers who go in for soul-cadences.*

Black rhythms and "soul-cheers" have dominated the pep rallies and the sports events. ("No, no, I don't think we'll be losin' our identity," a black matron in Georgia told Marshall Frady. "We're gonna give the whites a little soul. We're gonna give 'em some *tone*.") Not too long ago, a friend of mine named Eli Evans, traveling through the South doing work on a book, was driving down Main Street in Yazoo and saw some white cheerleaders practicing their yells in front of the Confederate monument. He got out of his car and listened for a while, and decided to bring me a gift back to New York. "All right, ladies, one more time," he said, turning on his tape recorder. "These aren't white girls," I told him, after we had played the tape in my office in New York. "Oh, yes, they are," Eli Evans said, producing a photograph he had taken of the cheerleaders to prove it. The white girls had rendered the old Yazoo yell, but the rhythms and indeed the very words themselves, I testify from my own

---

*As elsewhere in the South, Taylor High School, the former all-black high school, had its name changed, to "Yazoo City Junior High," and the athletic trophies which had been on display there were packed up and given to a former principal.

experience, were not what they were in the autumn of 1951.

Earlier, in the summer, two white students had written me a letter asking for my advice. They were trying to establish an integrated coffeehouse for high school students "to meet socially and just get to be friends," but the white adults were discouraging them at every turn. I did not know what to tell them. "The students are now just students," the letter had said. "If we can ever get around to knowing each other socially, it will help us all a lot. It's interesting to get to know them, but hard."

Now, in November, they told me what had happened. For a modest price, they had rented the boarded-up old building on Main Street which until quite recently had housed Tommy Norman's Drug Store, for years a unique and for all we knew a tenaciously permanent institution in Yazoo.* They offered "lifetime memberships" in the coffeehouse for 50 cents apiece, and a substantial number of white and black students wanted to join. They laid a new floor in Tommy Norman's and made plans to decorate the rest of it. "We wanted to get a place near the police station," a white boy said, "so we could tell our parents if anything went wrong, the police would be nearby."

There was considerable talk around town among

*For an earlier description of the interracial aspects of Tommy Norman's Drug Store when I was a boy, see pages 22-23.

the adults, especially when some parents discovered for what purposes the renovated Tommy Norman's would be used. The mayor, Jeppie Barbour, made several phone calls to white parents warning them of the integrated coffeehouse. Then the City Council condemned the building. Later the students talked with some white adults about renting them another building. No help was forthcoming.

PART THREE

1

I have a moviemaker friend in New York, a somewhat cranky and conservative exile from Louisiana, who told me he was emigrating to London. "It's not just the robots in the subways," he said, "or the surly manners, or the pollution, or the noise. I'm gettin' away from the spades."

I once lived in England for almost four years, I told him. He would love London for about six months, but after that it would start to get awfully boring.

"Why?" he asked. "Because after six months you'll start missing the spades," I said. He gave this some thought. "Well," he said, "you may be right."

This conversation took place shortly after I had published a magazine piece about the changes I had observed in Mississippi. My flamboyant and irascible friend, who had spent a considerable amount of time in Mississippi drinking mint juleps with the cousins of Sartorises and Compsons and de Spains and who was quite conversant with all the Southern literature, looked at me and began shaking his head. "You're crazy," he finally said, repeating it louder next time. *"Crazy!"* We were having a drink in the Empire Chinese bar on Madison, our magazine's hangout, and even the Chinese waiters—who by then were accustomed to strange outbursts from my steady clientele of writers, editors, agents, sexologists, sports columnists, mistresses to Black Panthers, advertising men, graduate students looking for scholarships with built-in retirement plans, hippie ministers, literary critics with socks that don't match, stylish poetesses in deep analysis since 1959, foreign correspondents, soil erosion experts, Russian émigrés, insurance salesmen, former advisors to Presidents, moderate revolutionaries (or makers of medium-sized fire bombs), ex-Existentialists, congressmen, draft dodgers, female political pundits, plantation owners, defrocked priests who live outdoors, and perambulating bums—turned their heads to listen. Mr. Suey Hom, the owner, came over and said, "Come on, let me buy you another drink, hah?"

"But this man is crazy," my companion persisted.

"Why is he crazy?" Mr. Suey wanted to know.

"Because he's a writer, but he wants to change Mississippi. Can you imagine? There he is with the most messed-up state in the Union, the most fertile ground in America for a writer to write about. The place of his own forebears. The most beautiful land in the whole damned country. The Goddamnedest people in the hemisphere, and all of them fucked up. Cruelties right out of the Old Testament. Relationships that would make Freud give up before he started. Emotions run wild. Romanticism gone amuck. Decadence. Decay. Incest. Filth. Complexity. Rank perversion. Miscegenation that is the envy of Brazil. Charm. Openness. The courage of noble fools. So much hospitality you have to beg them to stop. And he wants to *change* it. Why, if I was a writer I'd use all the influence I had with the politicians and get them to put up big-assed green signs at every point of entry into Mississippi, all along the borders, saying, 'Posted. No Trespassing.' "

I will have to admit that the dark and secret part of me was touched by this, and since my Louisiana friend had worked himself into a high fever, I told him so. "Besides," he said, "who gives a damn about the South any more? It's out of fashion everywhere. With these people it's up one year and down the next. They'll use it next time they need it. They've lost interest." He leaned across the table, narrowing his eyes conspiratorially, and whispered, *"But we know it's there, and that's where we've got the bastards beat."*

Who gives a damn about the South any more? Who, for that matter, gives a damn about integration? Back in the days of the Movement, that lost, lyrical time of innocence when the better part of the nation saw integration as the goal and fulfillment of our deepest impulses as a people, the South had once again been the symbol of our ills, the terrain on which to fight our noblest battles. To exorcise the South of its evils was to cleanse the nation of its simple politic hesitations. Then we could all go forward; we would overcome. But even before Martin Luther King was shot down in Memphis, articulate blacks were realizing Faulkner's prophesy—a prophesy everyone dismissed as garrulous eccentric racism when he said it years ago —that the real question might be not whether whites wanted to live with blacks, but precisely the other way around. The riots, the burnings, the embattled rhetoric; black studies, black separatism, Black Panthers. At times, the rest of America seemed more frightened than the South itself, whose bitter-enders could at the minimum take a simple metaphysical satisfaction in saying we told you so. Then the Eastern fashionmongering embraced the separatist apocalypse, and the radical chic made an avocation of violence, and the national Administration struck a deal with Strom Thurmond, and the Vice-President of the United States while dedicating the largest Confederate monument in Georgia decried forced intermingling, and even the more solid Northern intellectuals argued that racial integration was a false and remote intangible, and ordinary baffled white people almost everywhere said to hell with it. It was bone-chilling and shocking to ponder how the most powerful human commitments vanish with the styles in our country, and how the few very basic things which genuinely mattered (and there are not too very many) were lost or forgotten in the fire haze of benumbing words and histrionic gestures.

Integration. The very word seemed archaic and worn out, a little flighty and frivolous, and the silliest liberals seemed even sillier using it. Other, more pressing matters—the war, law and order, the battle of the generations—seemed to intervene. Just what did integration mean? Who cared about it now? Certainly not my friends in New York. How many genuine friendships between blacks and whites did I know here? As for the public schools, my own son was in a private school—with many blacks his age, of course, but private nonetheless—and so were the children of most of the people I knew. The hard-hat workers, suddenly the modish Forgotten Americans, had become more adept at race-baiting than the Southern rednecks, perhaps because they saw themselves more on television, and one could get from any New York cabdriver the three-minute lecture on inherent inferiority. It was all very mean, it did not do much to lift the soul, and yet in the North it was savageness with a faintly hollow and unhuman ring, a little too thought out and tawdry. Not of the flesh. Lacking the resonance of clashes of old armies. Bereft of guilt and curses of the blood. Removed from the Scriptures. Dislodged from memory. Stale with its cheap predictability. *Deracinated.* One night, driving in a cab on

Park Avenue with a friend from the South, the driver, Mr. Raccoli from the Bronx, had detected his accent and launched into a diatribe against blacks. It was the three-minute Bronx lecture. He paused for a sympathetic response. "If there's anything I can't stand," my friend drawled to the driver, "it's an amateur bigot."

The South had never been amateurish on these matters, indeed has been born and nurtured on them, but one had the feeling in 1970 that the venom had gone out of its segregationists, as if their previous unredeemable viciousness had become victim of the old vehemence itself, as if they had given too much of themselves to brutal and wearying battles consistently lost, even if to national ideals now gone a little murky and soft and ambivalent.* That was one thing. The other was so ironic, so utterly unexpected in the prevailing ambience that not too many Americans would fully comprehend: those who cared deepest and were working hardest for the true and just interracial society in America were the Southern white

*Lester Maddox in Georgia, for instance, had not been all that bad a governor. His brief Administration presided over the most sweeping racial changes in the history of the state. More important, the new governors elected in November, 1970, in Georgia, Florida, South Carolina, Tennessee, and Arkansas were rejecting the traditional appeals to regional and racial prejudice. Carter of Georgia: "The time for racial discrimination is over." West of South Carolina: "The politics of race and divisiveness . . . have been soundly repudiated." Askew of Florida: "We need improved economic opportunities for all our people, rural as well as urban, black as well as white." Even Wallace of Alabama seemed considerably milder.

moderates, and their ancient contemporaries, and the children of them both.

When school integration—the real article this time, not a sham retreat or a devious ploy—finally came to Mississippi and the South sixteen years after the *Brown* decision, a decision which had been hailed elsewhere as a judicial milestone, most of America neither saw its drama, forged as it was in the history and blood of a rich and tragic people, nor very much cared. For they had for an instant lost sight of certain true essentials: convinced themselves that the South was a backwater as soon as the complexity of the case was at their doorstep; frightened themselves away because—a harsh thing to say—the great black exodus to their cities had left them confused and despairing; listened, perhaps, to too much rhetoric about "relevance" in our times.

I was the editor of a national magazine, but I had been out and around the country in the late 1960s lecturing on the campuses: "to keep in touch," I told myself; to help pay New York alimony, I knew. Anyone who has done the lecture circuit will testify that it is wearying work, draining to the core, intensely and enervatingly lonely despite the vast unending wash of names and faces. But after a time I became not merely exhausted and used up. I had, as we used to say in college in the fifties, *had a crock:* with tweedy junior faculties and their morose and dumpy wives accosting the guest lecturer for deploring the notion of violence, of fashionable bloodthirsty talk, of the verbiage of doom and decay. *Had a crock* with the illiterate posturers, the fashionable young nihilists who told the same junior faculties that what they taught amounted to nothing, and the faculties agreed. *Had a crock* with all of them who erupted in spasms of irritated self-righteousness when they said that the South was all evil and could be written off, that black separatism was the wave of the future, that the Panthers should burn down every city in sight, that revolution was the hope of survival, that literature was useless because it no longer mattered to our condition. All this, and much more, would be spoken in the name of idealism. At one particularly raucous session (a "social" after an hour's talk, two weeks on the road), surrounded by academic revolutionaries and Panthers in leather jackets and grizzly long-hairs who seemed hot to burn some books, I said: "If Norman Mailer came from Brooklyn and became a Left Conservative, I came from Mississippi and have just become a States' Rights Democrat, and it is my privilege as a gentleman and dignitary to walk out of this convention." And I did. Never looking back till I got to New York.

One comes to learn much that is unexpected about the nation editing a serious magazine in New York. One tries to publish the best writing and journalism in America about the real problems besetting our country and our civilization: the terrible war, race, pollution, divisive leadership, drugs, and all the rest. At the same time, one must be very careful not to be washed into the backwaters by strong and immensely treacherous tides, for there is a treachery to intellectual faddishness and to the momentary voguish whim, and the stylish nonsense of one's own day can be quite terrible and brutalizing. Robert Penn Warren was speaking of writers when he accepted the National Medal for Literature, but it could just as easily have been of serious magazines, for what are magazines but writers? "It is hard to tell at any given moment what is relevant. The thing so advertised is likely to be as unrelated to reality as the skirt length is to the construction of the female anatomy—to be relevant merely to a symptom and not to a disease. The question is not that of the writer's own grounding in his time, the relation of his sensibility to his time, and paradoxically enough, of his resistance to his time. For there must be resistance, and the good work is always the drama of the writer's identity with, and struggle against, his time." In New York City itself, it was a time of extraordinary tensions in the intellectual life, the worst tensions since the thirties, the old heads said; everyone seemed at everyone else's throat; good manners themselves seemed a sign of weakness and retreat; righteousness and rudeness were traits to cultivate; categorizations and movements and harebrained commitments collided and reacted one to another, and everyone wanted good mileage out of something, or at the least three minutes on Cronkite or Brinkley. But so much of that which was inundating us—from Madison Avenue commercialism to East Side radicalism to the familiar unbending conservatism to the horrendous trend-making of the big media (and all those inane tracts of despair which more than ever before became best-sellers in suburban households)—all this ignored the immense diversity, darkness, and nobility of the nation, and threatened to do severe damage not only to the spirit and essence of literature itself, but to our living together with some reality and reason and civility.

One night in early 1970, I went to a fund-raising party on Park Avenue in Manhattan. Manhattan fund-raising parties are alien and berserk rituals unto themselves for those who do not know them, but this one was for the Reverend Andy Young, a young black from Georgia, a former close associate of Dr. King's who was running for Congress in Atlanta. Young had brought with him a sizable entourage of blacks from Georgia. These were men who had survived and indeed learned from the Movement, unlike many Southern blacks wasting away in the Village who had been casualties of it, fallen wounded to its promise and its failure. The party was in the home of a prominent black recording star, and Andy Young and the other Southerners were outnumbered, though not outclassed, by dozens of New York entertainers, bankers, PR men, advertisers, and full-time givers of New York parties. Andy Young gave a brief talk; much as I expected, it was intelligent, sensible, eminently humane, and funny, with an exceptional richness and understanding and complexity. I knew he was saying nothing here that he was not saying down in Georgia. Two or three of his Atlanta workers also spoke, and they were full of the rhythms and earthiness of Georgia, not to mention a fine professional awareness of its politics. They were able and strong, but I sensed they only used their powder when they knew the time was right, and when that happened one would be wary of brushing with them. Then the host stood up and launched into a tiresome rambling filibuster: bombastic, righteous, violent, fuzzy, ponderous, laden with disasters and seizures and relapses, devoid of ideas, much less of humanity. It was, to be specific, *gobbledygook.** Three of the co-hosts gave similar orations.† Halfway through the last one, I looked across the room, which was roughly

*The father of my friend Maury Maverick, Jr., coined this word when he was the leader of the F.D.R. liberal Turks in Congress in the early thirties. To him the word meant Manhattan talk: *gobbledygook.*

†I would remember something the Reverend James Bevel, another assistant to Martin Luther King, had said. "The Northern boys in the Movement never got a feeling for the South. . . . They thought that because black people in the South didn't spout off a lot of social philosophy they were stupid. Just because a man is out plowing with a mule doesn't mean he's a fool. It may mean he understands he's involved in a life process. . . . The Northern kids were being aggressive out of frustration, not out of wisdom."
—From *A Mind to Stay Here,* by John Egerton (New York: Macmillan, 1970).

the acreage of a football field, and saw a black Southerner from Alabama sulking behind the bar and
pouring himself a drink. We exchanged glances. A
few seconds later, right in the middle of the speech,
I heard my friend from Alabama shout, "Get him out
of there! Get the *Southerners* back up there. They're
the only ones makin' any *sense!*"

2

One of the more perplexing ironies of my life is that the longer I live in Manhattan, the more Southern I seem to become, the more obsessed with the old warring impulses of one's sensibility to be both Southern and American. It is an irony I take neither lightly nor fashionably; it is an honest obsession. Why, after all my generation of Americans has grown with in our coming to maturity—Auschwitz, Leningrad, Hiroshima, the Cold War, Vietnam, the assassinations of our finest young leaders, the enormous wastes and failures which haunt the greater American society—does this special part of America continue to engage my imagination, to touch me in the heart as no other can? Why, after seven years in Texas, three and a half in England and Europe, four as editor of a magazine with one of the most distinguished histories in the nation, am I still a son of that bedeviled and mystifying and exasperating region, and sense in the experience of it something of immense value and significance to the Great Republic? "Aren't we over all that shit?" a New Yorker asked me only a few nights ago.

Mississippi and Texas are the two places in America I know the best, or used to, yet even with Texas I find myself losing my old easy wonder and involvement. In the fifteen years since my friends and I on the student daily were censored by the established powers for concerning ourselves with issues which mattered in those days of McCarthy and Dulles, Texas at the true sources seemed to have changed hardly at all, so that after a time it struck one from afar who once cared deeply for its fractured, extravagant façades as a somewhat cheap and boring parody of itself. It lacked the blood and darkness and, yes, *character* of Mississippi, which despite its great despairs was slowly forming deeper strata, in torment and incertitude—deepening and extending itself toward something at once rich, various, and distinctive. Mississippi was maddened and bewitched; Texas, in its institutional aspects, was merely beholden, and as crude and self-satisfied as ever. Once again its state university was in the hands of the xenophobic knownothings, and the Texans who made the rules remained, toward the slightest hint of outside questioning, as everlastingly touchy and paranoiac as they had always been, spoiled grown adolescents who could take no way but their own. *"We're doin' all right. We've succeeded in runnin' out almost every-*

body down here like you," a powerful Texas wheeler-
dealer said to Bill Moyers in Austin. It all came down
to the quality of the money that controlled, and Texas
as a society, despite some of the most articulate dis-
senters in the nation, remained as firmly the domain
of the most uncivilized wealth in America as it had
been two generations before. So Texas seemed more
bereft than ever of that dark and brooding generosity
of the soul out of which the things that matter always
derive; it had not summoned the courage to try itself,
for in the end it had been corrupted and isolated by
nothing more complex than simple human greed,
and the noisy, stale narcissism that powerful and established greed entails.

But I am being unfair, and have not answered my
own question.

When I came up from the South by way of a Greyhound bus across the continent to work for the magazine I would later edit, I was in awe of it, just as I was
of the city itself, for all it had meant in our literature
to ambitious young outlanders such as I. I loved to
stand on balconies of apartments at the top of tall
buildings, tinkle the ice in my glass, and watch the
lights of the great city come on, as Tom Wolfe had,
and hear the light patter of cocktail talk among the
sleek, sophisticated people all around me; or to wan-
der its neighborhoods from Battery Park to Baker
Field on weekends; or to take a new issue of our maga-

zine the day it came off the press, hide in some bar by myself, and read it from cover to cover with a fine light glow of satisfaction and fulfillment; or to come to know the finest writers of one's day, to watch them as they finished some work which would be read a hundred years hence. One could come to terms with this extraordinary, driven, mad, and wondrous city if there were something to care for in it, something to engage one's calling and one's feeling for America.

Who, indeed, needed to be a Southerner? Here was the oldest journal in the nation, a durable old institution which had seldom hesitated to change as the times had changed, to speak in the accents of its own age. The pioneers had carried its bound volumes across the country in their covered wagons, and contemporary migrants from New England to Orange County, California, still carried them in the trunks of their Mustangs, Falcons, Cougars, Jaguars, and Barracudas. So a magazine became a living thing to me. Sometimes on rainy Saturdays, I would go to my office and take down from its library back issues a century old: to see what William Dean Howells had to say in 1898, or what the table of contents was in the issue which came out the month of my birth.* I would go to the file which had the records, card by card, of each story, article, or poem published since 1850, done al-

*It included pieces on the dangers of federal crime control, the Russian economy, population increases, and racism in America.

phabetically by the last name of the author, with the dates of acceptance and publication, the length of the manuscript, and the money paid. C: *Clemens, Samuel.* J: *James, Henry; James, William.* D: *Dickens, Charles.* E: *Eliot, George.* S: *Sartre, Jean Paul.* F: *Faulkner, William.* T: *Thackeray, W. M.* J: *Jones, James.* M: *Mann, Thomas.* R: *Roosevelt, Theodore.* K: *Kennedy, John F.; King, M. L.* C: *Crane, Stephen.* L: *Lewis, Sinclair.* P: *Porter, K. A.* K: *Kipling, Rudyard.* D: *Dickinson, Emily.* W: *Wilson, Woodrow.* All this was heady and exhilarating; it made me a little proud. Hundreds of letters, some of them hostile, most of them long and thoughtful, had come in after the publication of Norman Mailer's *Armies of the Night.* Mailer came to our office to read them. It took a few hours, but he looked over every one, and said: "All these people sitting all over America writing these letters. They're carrying on a conversation with a magazine as if a magazine itself were a human being."

It *was* a human being. At its best, it was encouraging and defending those of our contemporaries who were our best writers and journalists against the distractions and the philistinisms of modern America. It was seeking to draw on some of the flamboyance, the creativity, the richness of the language of the country. It was hoping to suggest that America still had the genius and courage to someday achieve its original promise as the hope of mankind. It had made mistakes. Sometimes it had gone too far, and at others it had said too little, but it was nothing if not American.

And it was to this city, whenever I went home, that I always knew I must return, for it was mistress of one's wildest hopes, protector of one's deepest privacies. It was half insane with its noise, violence, and decay, but it gave one the tender security of fulfillment. On winter afternoons, from my office, there were sunsets across Manhattan when the smog itself shimmered and glowed; later there would be long talks with colleagues, with gossip and plans for the next issue— *Vol. 241, No. 1450*—or how the cancellations stood in November as against the renewals, or when one of the writers would be back from Israel or California or Washington, or whether some others of them, whose deadlines were tomorrow, were drinking beer at this very instant at the Empire or at Greenstreet's. Despite its difficulties, which become more obvious all the time, one was constantly put to the test by this city, which finally came down to its people; no other place in America quite had such people, and they would not allow you to go stale; in the end they were its triumph and its reward.

The two places in America that more than any others are the nation writ large, as many an exile has finally discovered, are New York City and the South.

I go back to the South, physically and in my memories, to remind myself who I am, for the South keeps me going; it is an organizing principle, a feeling in the blood which pervades my awareness of my country and my civilization, and I know that Southerners are the most intensely incorrigible of all Americans. In the end, being what I am, I have no other choice; only New York could raise the question. When I am in the South and am driven by the old urge to escape again to the city, I still feel sorry for most of my contemporaries who do not have a place like mine to go back to, or to leave.

3

November 17, 1970

The last night I was in Mississippi, I had dinner with Hodding Carter III, editor of the paper in Greenville, the *Delta Democrat-Times*. Hodding's father, whom people call "Big Hodding" or sometimes just "Big," had retired now from the paper; he was one of my special heroes back when I was editing the daily at the University of Texas. Big Hodding had made a stop in Austin then on a lecture tour, and before an overflow crowd had said: "There is a young man from my native state who is the editor of your newspaper. It is an outstanding paper and he is doing a good job. All Mississippi boys are mean and rambunctious, so don't play around with him. He is in trouble now because all editors worthy of their calling get into trouble sooner or later." Then he proceeded from personal experience and with much gusto to defend the beleaguered notion of independent and courageous newspapers.

Shortly before I met young Hodding on my final night in Mississippi, I had driven from Jackson to Greenville for a visit in that remarkable, civilized river town. I had started out on the narrow old highway which parallels the river into the delta, and my rented Hertz had skidded and bumped all the way, and seemed to be balking a little at entering this ghostly terrain. Only a few miles into the delta, just as the sun disappeared out over the river, a storm descended, the rain came down in great torrents driven by a terrible whistling and moving wind, and beyond the edges of the highway I could see nothing but bayous and gullies and an occasional brutal little creek or river suddenly swollen and eddying with the rain. This, I knew from my boyhood, was one of the most desolate and treacherous drives in the whole state. My gasoline gauge pointed to empty, and I beseeched the Lord that I would not be stranded here in a storm, with not even a road shoulder to drive the car to, much less a Seven-Eleven or a Bun 'N Burger. I drove for miles in a mindless fright until, praise eternally be His name, there was the town of Onward, Mississippi, with a general store plastered with patent-medicine posters and a gas pump sitting precariously on the edge of the swamp. Back in the car again, stopping every so often to read in the eerie glow of the headlights the historical markers about the early Indians, the Spanish explorers, or the French settlers, I felt for the hundredth time the pull of that powerful and unremitting delta land, its abiding mysteries and strengths—retrieved from the ocean and later the interminable swamp—and the men of all colors and gradations known to the species who had fought it into its reluctant and tentative submission. No wonder there is no other state remotely like this one, I thought, no other so eternally wild, so savagely unpredictable, so fraught with contradictory deceits and nobilities; societies are shaped by the land from which they emerge, and on this night in a dark and relentless November storm, the land from which I and my blood-kin had emerged was scaring the unholy hell out of me.

Now young Hodding and I were in the old Southern Tearoom in Vicksburg, being served catfish by Negro mammies dressed for the role, only a few hundred yards from the great battlefield where 20,000 American boys—average age 20—died in Vicksburg's gullies and ravines and swamps 107 years before. We had refused the "Yazoo Razoo," the "Mississippi Grasshopper," and the "Rebel on the Rocks" and had settled down with some serious Yankee Martinis. Hodding and I are almost precisely the same age, but he came back and I went away, so we approach our common place like two radiants in the same prism, but with the same impetuosity, and the same maniacal blend of fidelity, rage, affection, and despair. I had my plane out the next day, and so I was loosening up with no effort at all, for now as always I felt, on the eve of departure, the lifting of some terrible burden, almost physical in its intensity. I had been back six times since my first trepidations about death on native soil; I had not been murdered, had not been shot at, had not even been treated rudely or narrowly, as I should have had the good sense to know all along; my Manhattan premonition was in truth the old endemic heart's fear of too deep an involvement in this place I came out of, where by the simple pristine intensity of emotion, the people in it have always been somewhat more than human to me, and hence confront me nostril-to-nostril with my own humanity.

A few days before, Hodding had been jumped, for the first time in a long while, by some hard-noses in a restaurant in Greenville called Doe's. There were five of them—from Prentiss, Mississippi, it turned out —and they had asked him over to their table. *"So you're Hodding Carter,"* one of the hard-noses said, with a sneer from his lips to the beginning of his left ear lobe. Hodding had tried to be friendly, in a kind of collegiate Southern way, a rather tentative amalgam of Princeton and Greenville High School: to kill them, as we are taught here, with kindness, "because," he said later, "people like that down here are worth winning over." But within earshot of his beautiful blond wife Peggy, sitting at his table, they had called him a "mother-fucker," "son of a bitch," and "nigger-lover," and perhaps even accused him of being out for the Yankee dollar. There is a certain strain of violence in Hodding's molecular composition. Most of his qualities derive from gentlemanly sources, but a remaining few have some remembrance of precisely what it took in blood for the rest to be gentlemanly; so beneath the dark good looks and the Mississippi charm, there is a lurking touchy quality, as in me, that would allow him to damage a man very badly if he lost part of the prepossession they taught him in Old Nassau Hall. But this time there were five of them, and he was with his wife, so he left, feeling a little guilty for leaving, saying, "If I were in the kind of shape I was in when I was in the Marines . . . ," but still not too proud of the encounter, and even less so when his wife got an obscene phone call that night from one of them.

He had once told me that when he took over the paper from his father several years before and got the usual threatening letters and phone calls, he would sometimes spend all night in the shrubs in front of his house with a gun. Or he would put a strip of Scotch tape on the crack of the hood of his car, and check each morning to see if it had been broken. He was even reluctant to go out into the little towns of the delta, the same dusty hamlets where I had been knocked around, often humiliated spiritually as well as manhandled physically, when playing sports in high school. Now he no longer sits in the shrubs or

e and this involvement in a common history
ry of anguish and cruelty and inhumanity,
f courage and warmth and rare nobility—is
heir fellow Americans of the terrible toll
rness and retreat can take; for this will give
n some feel of itself, and help it to endure.

t, Long Island

18, 1971

bothers with the Scotch tape, and he goes out into the little delta towns all the time on stories or to give speeches. He is a friend of Charles Evers, Aaron Henry, and the Negro leadership; he edits the best paper in Mississippi and one of the best in the South; he is blood-proud and quirky, with a high quotient for recognizing nonsense in whatever form it comes his way. "Mississippi by any human measure has had to reform," he once said. "But in the very process of reforming, and all that that entails, we may become like the rest of the country." Adding: "You're obsessed with the South and went away. I'm not and I stayed."

"It's *insane,*" Hodding was saying, having previously lied to me that he had an uncle and a grandfather who fell here at Vicksburg, carrying tattered flags punctured with several dozen miniballs and riddled with New Jersey canister. *"Mississippi!* The one very damned place where Yankees and everybody else say this can't work, and it's become the battlefront. It's part of the screwy system in this nation that the one state least equipped, financially and emotionally, to deal with all the implications of it is finally havin' to do it first.

"People like Satterfield could have helped us, maybe could have saved us with their impeccable white Mississippi credentials. They could have helped move things in a civilized way, but they took their refuge in the thickets of the law. One thing's for sure, there won't be any flight to white suburbia down here. Where do you go? Hollandale? It's 80 per cent black. Itta Bena? It's more. I've got cousins up in Scarsdale who are very happy."

Why, then, did it finally get here first? Now he gesticulates a little, raising his voice, and the Negro mammies look over our way, and for all I know even some of the rotted gray ghosts of our people in the big cemetery up the river bluffs. "Through *stupidity! Sheer stupidity.* Sheer *unyielding conservatism!* That's why. All the state had to do was talk quietly and try to accommodate, and be a typical hypocritical American state. But there's no halfway measures in *this* place." He flourished his knife at the catfish. "Hell, it just might work here someday. Wouldn't *that* surprise 'em?"

Now the oracles sitting in the Georgetown precincts of Washington would have us rest in peace. Stewart Alsop writes in *Newsweek* that "integration is a failure . . . it has become impossible to hide from view any longer the fact that school integration, although it has certainly been 'an experiment noble in purpose,' had tragically failed about everywhere." The crafty and cynical policy of the Nixon Administration would give further endorsement to what the disillusioned Yankee liberals and the Northern black separatists have given their benediction, not to so much as suggest all the racists everywhere. It takes a Southerner to know the extent to which the South has

always been the toy ar
righteousness, of all th
tive of the national gui
nation's oscillations o
trenchments. The Yan
always been the wors
absenteeism was the
from our most difficu

I believe that what
town with less of a
apartment complexe
Island will be of end
is people trying: lo
and perpetrating th
dramatized by our l
best instincts only
may fall before an
are mature enough
how thin is the skei
less these instincts
all. How many otl
have done nearly
share a rootedness
pain we have bee
the South—all of
tin Compson spe
Canadian roomn
hate it, and we c
the burdens of th

this plac
—a histo
but also
to warn
that bitte
the natio

Wainscot

January

AFTERWORD

I still have the June 1970 issue of *Harper's Magazine* with its iconic cover—a full-bleed close-up of the rear end of a yellow school bus, as if the reader is following too close behind it. "Willie Morris in Mississippi," the heading reads. I had eagerly awaited this issue because it featured my adopted new home-town, Yazoo City, and the desegregation of the high school where I had taught for three years.

This was Willie Morris's town, too, and his school. Willie was Yazoo's most famous and controversial son, the topic of heated conversations ever since I moved there as a newlywed in 1965. I had met Willie when he came to the high school and read from his forthcoming book, *North Toward Home*, and my hus-band and I were among those who enjoyed Willie's company on his occasional visits home. Twenty years later I would become Willie's wife, but such a notion was outside anyone's imagination then. Even now, as I recall that time and place, I am stunned by the sneaky ways of fate.

A product of the segregated society of the Mississippi Delta, I entered Ole Miss with James Meredith in 1962. In Yazoo City in 1968 my friend and fellow teacher Harriet DeCell and I volunteered, under

the court's "Freedom of Choice" plan, to teach at the
all-black high school, the only white teachers to do so.
The following year we added a black teacher to our
team. Teaching had deeply enriched my sensibilities
and expanded my view of things. I had no doubt that
integration would work in Yazoo City. That was
Willie's judgment, too. In *Yazoo: Integration in a
Deep-Southern Town* (reprinted here), an expanded
treatment of the magazine article, Willie explores the
idea of redemption and racial reconciliation in his
beloved and troubled Deep South, a theme he would
revisit in his writing throughout his life.

When Willie researched and wrote about the
desegregation of the Yazoo City schools in 1970, he
stood at the pinnacle of a brilliant career as an editor
and journalist. He had *made* it in New York. His
accelerated rise in American journalism and the New
York cultural scene is a mythic American tale—small-
town kid makes it big in the big city.

Willie's journey fits the script perfectly. He was a
bright and affable boy who loved sports and pranks
and his dog named Skip. After high school, he
attended the University of Texas and became the
intrepid editor of the student newspaper, challenging
the Texas Board of Regents on the paper's First
Amendment rights. Selected as a Rhodes Scholar, he
studied at Oxford University, returning in 1960 to edit
the freewheeling liberal weekly, the *Texas Observer*.

In 1963 Willie rode a Greyhound bus across the

country to take a job as an associate editor of *Harper's Magazine*, a sedate, respectable literary journal.

Four years later, at the age of thirty-two, he became editor-in-chief and transformed it, overnight it seemed, into a high-spirited and edgy political and cultural magazine that published seminal articles of American journalism written by the finest writers in the country. It was Willie's *Harper's* that published Seymour Hersh's "My Lai Massacre," Norman Mailer's "Armies of the Night," Bill Moyers's "Listening to America," David Halberstam's trenchant pieces on the Vietnam War, and excerpts from such literary classics as William Styron's *Confessions of Nat Turner* and Maya Angelou's *I Know Why the Caged Bird Sings*.

The novelist William Styron described Willie's editorship at *Harper's*: "I can't imagine a more glorious time for writers and journalists, than the frenzied last years of the '60s when Willie, a mere kid, was guiding *Harper's Magazine* with such consummate skill and imagination . . . the wise aplomb of an editorial master, and for several golden years his creation was the preeminent journal in the nation, not only its keenest observer of political and social affairs but its most attractive literary showcase."

Fast forward to 1996 at Elaine's, the fabled New York hangout for writers, actors, and assorted others. It was Willie's favorite spot when he lived in New York. We were hosting a dinner for Rob Reiner and a few others who were in town for the premiere of the film, *Ghosts of Mississippi*, about the prosecution and conviction of the man who murdered civil rights leader Medgar Evers in 1963. My dinner partner on this occasion was John Kennedy Jr., whose new magazine *George* had just published Willie's piece about the making of that movie. Early in the evening, John leaned in to tell me that when he first talked with his mother about starting a magazine, she gave him a copy of the one book that he must read: It was *New York Days* by Willie Morris.

But that evening was many years after Willie's glorious New York days had ended. The Mississippi rebel clashed irrevocably with the conservative owners of *Harper's Magazine*. When Willie resigned, his writers did, also, in outraged solidarity. *Yazoo: Integration in a Deep-Southern Town* came out in the spring of 1971, at the very time he was ending his tenure at *Harper's*. It seems fitting that, as *Yazoo* tells a story of social transformation, this book stands at the juncture of a major shift in Willie's life: from editor and journalist to writer. After flourishing in the epicenter of the biggest happenings in the country and the world's most interesting people, he turned to one of the most solitary of occupations. There were other possibilities, job offers, in publishing, television, politics. But Willie ignored or declined them all. He would find his own way, somehow, as a writer. His next journey was uncharted and much less secure.

From 1971 until his death in 1999, Willie wrote books—twenty in all—and essays by the hundreds, for magazines and newspapers and the books of others. These years fall conveniently into three decades in three different places: the 1970s in eastern Long Island; the 1980s in Oxford, Mississippi; the 1990s in Jackson, Mississippi.

At the end of his tenure at *Harper's,* shaken by the swift turn of events, Willie retreated to eastern Long Island for much-needed rest and recovery. There he found the embrace of old friends and the welcome of new ones: literary and publishing types escaping the city on weekends and in the summer, writers and their families, actors, artists, potato farmers, and shopkeepers. Always one to make friends easily, he was soon a familiar presence in the village of Bridgehampton. As he had at Elaine's, Willie quickly settled in many nights at Bobby Van's in Bridgehampton.

During the day, he wrote many articles and four books. His first book, *Good Old Boy,* is an enduring Tom Sawyer–like adventure story for young adults, in which Willie embellishes his own boyhood with strands of local history and lore. Near the end of his Long Island period, he wrote *James Jones: A Friendship,* a biographical memoir about the author of *From Here to Eternity.* Personal and evocative like his other nonfiction works, this book begins with reflections on his own mother's death and ends at the graveside of Jones.

Mississippi was always in Willie's rearview mirror. He continued to visit Yazoo City for family and professional reasons, arriving with other national media to cover President Carter's Yazoo City town meeting for *Time* magazine. He wrote a lyrical introductory essay for the history of Yazoo County written by Harriet and me; and he came down from Long Island to sign books at our big publication party. I was pleased and but a little surprised, too, that he took the time to do it. It was my first realization that the essence of Willie's charm was his generosity. When Ole Miss offered him a position as creative writing teacher and writer-in-residence, he did not hesitate. In January 1980 he loaded up his car with his books and papers and his black lab Pete and headed south to Oxford, Mississippi. Ole Miss and Willie Morris were a match. His presence on the campus represented the university's confirmation that its defiant past was behind it. Willie lured many of his literary friends to teach or speak on campus and sometimes taught his own classes downtown at a favorite gathering place. Plus, there were pretty girls everywhere he looked and Ole Miss football every fall!

If Long Island had been about rest and recovery, Oxford was about reconciliation and renewal. Willie was elated to discover a new Mississippi led by the erudite and progressive governor William Winter, and one that welcomed its exiled son home. "Here I was back in the deep dark womb of home," he wrote in *New York Days*. "The eternal juxtaposition of . . . hate and love, the apposition of its severity and tenderness, would forever baffle and enrage me . . . but these forever drive me to words. Meanness is everywhere, but here the meanness and the desperation and the nobility have for me their own dramatic edge, for the fools are my fools and the heroes are mine, too."

During the 1980s Willie published seven books of nonfiction, including *The Courting of Marcus Dupree*, an award-winning book about an African American high school football player in Neshoba County, Mississippi, the place where only a generation before, three young civil rights activists had been savagely murdered. In this book, Willie examines the state's past and the terrible burden of race as he shows how football and local pride in a black teenager brings the black and white communities together.

The publication of a slim collection of Willie's essays by the University Press of Mississippi changed his life, and my own as well. The book was *Homecomings*, and I was its editor, having left teaching to join the editorial staff at the university press in Jackson. I signed Willie to do the book and he turned in his manuscript a year later, right on time. It was a professional deal just like the other twenty or so books I acquired each year. As we moved toward the publication date, however, our editorial conferences become more frequent and our phone calls less literary. The book was published in the fall of 1989, became a bestseller within the state, and received critical acceptance outside of it. Willie proposed to me at a publication party a few months later in the U.S. Senate Caucus Room in Washington, in front of two thousand guests. We were married in September 1990, and Willie moved to Jackson.

One day Willie pulled from the bookshelf my Yazoo County history for which he had written the introduction, the very copy he had inscribed at the Yazoo City library those many years before. Both of us were astonished and amused as he read aloud what he had written: "Dearest JoAnne, You and Harriet in this book have done one of the most valuable, beautiful things this place has known, and as you grow older, you will acknowledge this. I applaud you and love you for the care, discipline, and talent to have done it. Besides, you're beautiful and a great teacher. Love, Willie."

How do I describe Willie's Jackson years, the ones I know best of all? A friend suggested "rebirth" or even "reincarnation." But the word that comes most vividly to my mind is *fulfillment*. The Willie I knew in his last decade was fulfilled. Not that he was satisfied by his accomplishments, but that he was fully engaged in every moment, creatively engaged, engrossed in his work and in every phase of his life. He was writing well and publishing good books, *New York Days* and *My Dog Skip* among them. His discipline and consistency amazed and impressed me. Willie's haphazard mode of dress and well-known affinity for late nights and brawny beverages have suggested, incorrectly, to some that Willie was disorganized, his work in disarray. In fact, Willie had an orderly mind and well-ordered, even methodical, work habits. His desk was organized and tidy, and he kept regular work hours—four or five hours every afternoon.

In the evenings at the end of a productive day at his desk, Willie loved nothing better than going out to a favorite local restaurant with his wife and good friends and, on occasion, entertaining fans who gathered around his table to enjoy his repartee and bottomless reservoir of stories. Some of his finest, most fulfilling moments were those spent talking to young (and not-so-young) people who had ideas and a longing to write. With genuine interest and an attentive ear, he would learn their life stories, discerning with astonishing, almost mystical, clarity their dreams and insecurities, encouraging or challenging them—inspiring them—to think and write and follow their heart. I saw this phenomenon occur not once but many times. In the hundreds of letters I received after Willie's death, from his friends, students, and mere acquaintances across the years, I read again and again of such encounters from those who said that, with only a few words, which they recounted verbatim, "Willie changed my life."

Among his most lasting legacies are the many books of writers who have written and published fine books because of Willie's encouragement or support. Ed Yoder, his good friend since their Rhodes days in England, has written of this marvelous capacity of Willie's:

> Those who were not only Willie's friends but writers also knew that Willie watched over them and their work from any distance, like a literary guardian angel . . . He poured great energy into matching writers with their proper subjects and destinies; destinies he often saw more clearly and quickly than they. . . . He planted the seed, or edited a manuscript, or conceptualized an as yet unarticulated book, or encouraged reluctant writers to mine their hidden strengths.

Willie reveled in the symmetry of living late in life in the city of his birth, where his grandparents Mamie and Percy, and his two great-aunts had lived, where he spent every Christmas Day and so many lazy summer days, riding forty miles south on the Greyhound. On weekends Willie and I often drove the streets of old and new Jackson, searching for the sites of his boyhood memories. Sometimes we took the back roads to Yazoo City just to see who came in on the Amtrak that day or who had been recently buried in the cemetery. These were quiet, easy, often reflective times when Willie reminisced and pondered the vicissitudes of life.

One topic that bewildered him was the outcome of desegregation in the Yazoo schools, which he had written about with such conviction and optimism. I had continued teaching in the Yazoo City public schools until the early 1980s; my two sons attended Yazoo's public elementary and middle schools, so I had a front-row seat when it came to judging the success of integration. I saw it working. Sometime in the mid- to late eighties, however, white students began transferring, in increasing numbers each year, to private all-white academies, eventually bringing about the *re*segregation of that deep-southern town.

"I was wrong. In my book *Yazoo*, I got it wrong," Willie said later. It was more than a mere statement of fact; it was an implicit plea for answers: Why had school integration failed in Yazoo City after such a hopeful beginning? How had he been so wrong about the Yazoo people? What happened?

Willie did not live long enough to find satisfactory answers to these questions, nor, to my knowledge, has anyone else. Resegregation has occurred not only in the Yazoo City but in schools across the country, for reasons known and unknown. Do the causes vary from place to place? Are there common threads? What does it all mean? The answers are out there in Yazoo and elsewhere, awaiting scholars and writers with the courage and passion and tenacity to unearth them and write their books. A guardian angel is expecting them.

JOANNE PRICHARD MORRIS